# Hispanic Roots of the Hollywood Western

# Hispanic Roots of the Hollywood Western

Mimi Reisel Gladstein and Susana Lozano

Fort Worth, Texas

Library of Congress Cataloging-in-Publication Data

Names: Gladstein, Mimi Reisel, author. | Lozano Moreno, Susana, 1956- author.
Title: The Hispanic roots of the Hollywood Western / by Mimi Reisel Gladstein and Susana Lozano.
Description: Fort Worth : TCU Press, [2024] | Includes bibliographical references and index. | Summary: "Hispanic Roots of the Hollywood Western explores how the Spanish history of the American Southwest influenced a movie genre that became a worldwide phenomenon: the Western. Numerous aspects of the Hispanic heritage of the Old West appear in Westerns, including Spanish-language place names, Spanish architecture, and Hispanic characters. This book explores these elements through the lens of two archetypal Western protagonists: the Cisco Kid and Zorro. These two characters starred in books, radio shows, and movies throughout the twentieth century, eventually becoming a natural part of American popular culture. They sometimes acted as heroes, sometimes as antiheroes, but in both cases, they helped to create a joyful and positive image in the American collective unconscious of what it meant to be Hispanic in the Wild West. These representations are part of the American cinematographic legacy; to forget them would be to lose a part of our collective identity. Exploring the Hispanic origins of early Westerns is also key to understanding Westerns that came later, such as Sergio Leone's films and Clint Eastwood in his poncho. The role played by Spain itself continued to be significant, as multiple locations (including Madrid, Barcelona, and Almería) were converted into shooting locations for Westerns throughout the 1950s-1970s. Some of these films were internationally recognized as universal masterpieces of cinematography, like the Dollars Trilogy. This book is essential not only for anyone interested in the origins and development of Westerns, but also for those who are interested in what meant to be Hispanic in the Far West in past centuries, and what it means to be American today"-- Provided by publisher.
Identifiers: LCCN 2024044567 (print) | LCCN 2024044568 (ebook) | ISBN 9780875658919 (paperback) | ISBN 9780875659015 (ebook)
Subjects: LCSH: Western films--United States--History and criticism. | Hispanic Americans in motion pictures. | National characteristics, American, in motion pictures. | Heroes in motion pictures. | Motion pictures and history. | Western films--Influence. | West (U.S.)--In motion pictures. | United States--Civilization--Spanish influences. | LCGFT: Film criticism.
Classification: LCC PN1995.9.W4 G58 2024 (print) | LCC PN1995.9.W4 (ebook) | DDC 791.43/658780973--dc23/eng/20241030
LC record available at https://lccn.loc.gov/2024044567
LC ebook record available at https://lccn.loc.gov/2024044568

TCU Box 298300
Fort Worth, Texas 76129
www.tcupress.com

Design by Bill Brammer

*Dedicated to:*

*Jay Gladstein*

*Antonio Drove*

*Fernando Rodríguez Melchior*

# Contents

# Introduction

MUCH HAS BEEN WRITTEN about the sources and inspirations that formed the foundation of what is often considered the most American film genre: the Western. In their introduction to *Western Movies*, Pilkington and Graham call them "America's unique contribution to that body of mythic lore familiar to most of the human race."

To begin, it is important that we clarify our use of certain terminology in this study. What a group is called or how a group is identified is the topic of much conflict, particularly in this era of post-civil-rights struggles. It is not our purpose here to engage in those linguistic political battles. In his choice of terminology for *Latino Images in Film*, Charles Ramirez Berg rejects the term "Hispanic" as "imprecise and bureaucratic," choosing the term "Latino" instead. For his purposes he chooses to use "Latino" as an "umbrella term for people of Latin American descent," in which he includes all citizens of Central and South America. His point was that, as Hollywood in its stereotyping did not differentiate among those different nationalities—making no distinction, for instance, between Mexicans and Mexican-Americans—neither would he for his discussion. This study, however, will use the term "Hispanic" as a more precise way of identifying the groups we are referencing: the Spanish and their descendants in Mexico. In his mural in the National Palace in Mexico City, Diego Rivera included La Malinche, holding a blue-eyed baby. When local guides point out this part of the mural, they often refer to this as the "first Mexican." While the racial classification of Mexicans varies, the largest portion are *mestizo*, or mixed race. More often than not, this means a Spanish and Indigenous mix. This is particularly true in that area of what is now the United States that was explored and settled by the conquistadors.

Needless to say, the dominant language of Mexico, the West, and Southwest until the nineteenth century was Spanish. A political irony is that whereas English replaced Spanish in what came to be part of the United States during the late nineteenth and throughout the twentieth century, Spanish is once more a dominant language in the twenty-first century in these areas (a region often referred to as Aztlan).

Again, since our purpose is to transmit a historical narrative, we will use the terms "Native American" and "Indian" interchangeably when referring to the members of the various Indigenous tribes that inhabited Mexico and the West and Southwest of what became the United States. Though "Indian" is a misnomer, used only because Columbus thought he had reached India, it was the contemporary term in use for much of the time that we will be writing about. When young children would don their feathered headdresses and carry their store-bought bow and arrows, while their friends buckled on a holster and cap-pistol and pretend Stetson, they called their play "cowboys and Indians." Even in Spain, children call this game "jugar a indios y vaqueros [playing cowboys and Indians]." For much of the time, in the movies we will be discussing, whether the individual was a member of the Sioux, Apache, or Arapaho tribe, the term used to describe him or her was "Indian." We will therefore use this term where historically appropriate, such as in direct quotations.

Since our study is about roots, its structure is necessarily historical. Therefore, we begin with the notion that Spain provided the essential foundation for that which we think of as the "West." Landing first in Mexico, Spanish explorers and missionaries were the first Europeans in Texas, New Mexico, Arizona, Nevada, and California, the primary locations and settings for Western movies. Spain had a three hundred–year head start in terms of dominating the culture of that part of the world. This is not to make any political point but to explain our use of the term "Hispanic," in that we will be discussing Spain and its colony Mexico. When Mexico won its independence, Spanish influence did not end. The principal Spanish religion, Catholicism, with its churches and steeples, remained dominant. In addition, the architecture and village structure or layout, around a central plaza, remains. The majority of family names derive from Spain. The dances and the music of Mexico owe much to the influence of Spain, as does the musical dominance of the guitar. And of course, although there are some regional differences, as in any language, still the language remains the same: Spanish is the official language of Mexico.

An important caveat is our desire to avoid engaging in the discussion of the issue of what Francis M. Nevins calls "the gringos who . . . hired other gringos to play dress-up with bolero jackets and big sombreros . . . [and portray Latinos as] a bunch of fat, lazy, dirty, ignorant greasers with ragged mustaches who couldn't speak an English sentence without turning it into taco meat."

Let us also make clear at the onset that this study was not meant to be encyclopedic. We cannot possibly cover all the instances in Western movies, whether made in Hollywood or elsewhere, that provide evidence of Hispanic roots. However, this study is calibrated to add a needed dimension to the story of what Anthony Mann calls this "most popular and long-lasting genre." This need is evidenced by the fact that in some of the books that purport to tell the story of the Western, significant Hispanic pioneer figures such as Zorro and the Cisco Kid are either ignored or mentioned only in a footnote. Mary Lea Bandy and Kevin Stoehr's *Ride, Boldly Ride: The Evolution of the American Western* excludes any mention of Zorro; Cisco is only noted in one sentence about sidekicks, which mentions that many sidekicks like Pancho are "Spanish" or Native American. Other than that, the only other reference is in an endnote. Although Warner Baxter's portrayal of the Cisco Kid won an Academy Award in 1929, George N. Fenin and William K. Everson's *The Western: From Silents to the Seventies* does not cover this significant Western, and their discussion of Douglas Fairbanks dismisses his *Mark of Zorro* as a costume drama. It is our expectation that the reader will be able to add many instances we were unable to cite.

Though our study is not meant to be encyclopedic, that does not diminish the importance of the Western in the history of how American identity was built. Written narratives throughout time share a common trajectory: most cultures start creating their identity around glorious stories of the heroes of "their group," narrating epic adventures that allow the group to feel proud of themselves. In this vein we could include, for example, the origins of British-English identity in *Beowulf* and the rise of the Spanish identity through *Cantar de Mio Cid*. These represent two main works among thousands of stories that represent a genre: the epic.

This happened long ago in the Old World, but immigrants to the New World had to follow these same steps more recently to create their identity and had to sing of the adversities that their people had to face in the building of their culture and their nation. This is why, when Americans started writing and filming, many of them told stories of the heroes and the people who went westward, creating this genre named the "Western." The history of Americans is the history of people always going westward: some of them from the Old World to the New World, and some of them just going west within the New World. This genre tells stories about those "who went West": how they lived, who they were, and who their heroes and villains were. Thus, though some may have dismissed this genre as something unimportant, since to a great part of the populace Western books and films are considered lowbrow and cheap, it is a crucial genre, as it constitutes the original epic of American culture.

So, the epic narrative that we find only within American civilization constitutes this genre we call "Western": the American epic. With this understanding, we can state that a film such as *The Man Who Shot Liberty Valance* is as meaningful and beautiful as *Beowulf* or *Cantar de Mio Cid*, the three of them being clear epic exponents of their respective cultures and identities.

All cultural identities need a kind of "Olympus" (as a metaphor of all cultures' mythical territory) to identify all the myths that comprise their collective imaginary, and most of the myths that inhabit the "American Olympus" were produced in the Western universe. These myths are the "net" of archetypes that constitute the group, the whole culture that can see "itself" reflected or projected on that "Olympus." But this mythical territory, to be satisfying and fulfilling, has to include all the members of the group, leading with a legendary past that mythically portrays our ancestors, showing us where we come from. In this sense, as important as *The Man Who Shot Liberty Valance* is the Western *In Old Arizona*, not only because it is a great film, but also because it socially and culturally provides the American culture with a character (an archetype of an ancestor inhabiting the "American Olympus") that allows American society to recognize Hispanic heroes among the heroes of the Western epic.

We cannot do less than ponder deeply and rigorously the roots of the American Westerns, as, knowing and considering them, we will find the very roots of what being American means.

Chapter 1

# American Epic Heroes and Antiheroes

FACING DIACHRONICALLY how American Western heroes have been traditionally understood, we find that the most dominant image is the one that links the American epic hero with an individualist, brave, Caucasian man, who may be the origin of what finally became, as time passed by, the self-made man, in both the countryside and in the cities.

This hero is white and ambiguously a descendant of Western-Central Europeans. Nevertheless, probably most of them have an English heritage if we consider their names, aspects, and resemblances. This English heritage means coming not only from England but also from wherever the English language is spoken in Europe: England, Ireland, Scotland, or Wales. Fulfilling this description, we find the best well-known actors who have played Western heroes in films: James Stewart, John Wayne, Gary Cooper, Henry Fonda, Burt Lancaster, Kirk Douglas, Robert Mitchum, Rock Hudson, Paul Newman, Steve McQueen, and Clint Eastwood. This is the archetype we have in mind when we think of a cowboy, a sheriff, a ranch owner, etc.

They are tall, slender, most of them blue-eyed, rustic but educated, restrained, and with a deep sense of fairness. They are brave and ready to fight for the weak, no matter if no one else will help them. They are usually poor and not ambitious, and their only concern is to live peacefully and freely. These are the "good cowboys," the "good sheriffs," that is to say, the traditional epic heroes of Westerns, riding a horse and with a gun always at the ready to enact justice.

Nobody knows, within most of these Western plots, where these fictional heroes come from and where they go, and much less who their parents were. We only know that their fictional names make their English heritage explicit: Ransom Stoddard and Tom Doniphon (*The Man Who Shot Liberty Valance*); Cole Thornton (*El Dorado*); Ethan Edwards (*The Searchers*); Ringo Kid (*The Stagecoach*); Lt. Col. Kirby Yorke (*Rio Grande*); Sheriff John T. Chance (*Rio Bravo*); Marshal Will Kane (*High Noon*); Jethro Stuart, Linus Rawlings, and Mike King (*How the West Was Won*); Bannock Marshal Jared Maddox (*Lawman*); William J. Tadlock and Dick Summers (*The Way West*); Matt Calder (*River of No Return*); Jordan Benedict Jr. (*Giant*); Bill Munny (*Unforgiven*), etc. And when the story starts, it is common to find them "wandering," which is to say "in movement": they are arriving somewhere or going from one place to another.

But this image of the Western hero is incomplete, as they are not the only American epic heroes, both in reality and in fiction. There are other American Western epic heroes who are very different from those we have already mentioned. These Western heroes are also at the roots of this epic American genre and are still "alive" nowadays in contemporary books, films, and even comics and videogames. They are the Western heroes with Spanish heritage. The actors who played this second type are Warner Baxter, Cesar Romero, Duncan Renaldo, Gilbert Roland, Douglas Fairbanks, Reed Hadley, Tyrone Power, Alain Delon, and Antonio Banderas, most of them playing the roles of two very meaningful characters: Cisco Kid and Zorro.

So, we can establish that there are two main hero archetypes within American Westerns: the ones with English heritage and the ones with Spanish heritage.

And it is not meaningless that the first Western that won an Oscar featured a Spanish-heritage hero: Cisco Kid. *In Old Arizona* (1929), directed by Irving Cummings and Raoul Walsh, was nominated for five Academy Awards—including Best Picture—at the 1928–1929 Academy Awards. Warner Baxter, playing the Cisco Kid, won the Academy Award for Best Actor.

Taking into account this hero archetype within Westerns is

important not only for the history of Westerns but also—as we have pointed out—culturally and socially for many Americans. Properly identifying these heroes within Westerns will mean that those Americans with a Spanish heritage will recognize their ancestors as American epic heroes, as those coming from an English heritage already do. This is something that will allow millions of Americans with a Spanish heritage to identify themselves with a "hero" and not have to look at themselves in the past as those Hispanics who appear in some films as "fat, lazy, dirty, ignorant, greasers with ragged mustaches," in the words of Francis M. Nevins.

The Hispanic Western hero is an archetype that has been neglected—when not ignored or disdained—by the traditional historical studies on Westerns, devoting to them only a few lines or even none, as if they were second-class heroes, most times disregarded by principles. This becomes outrageously obvious when we compare the existing bibliography on this issue: while the one based on the English-heritage archetype is huge, studies on the Spanish-heritage archetype are very rare. This is an oversight that this study tries to contribute to remedying.

Both are American heroes, born in America, but with a different presence in our collective perception and with diverse personalities emerging from their dissimilar origins. Both hero archetypes have common features, of course, but they are distinct. It is very interesting to compare them, as many clues to American identity emerge from their comparison. Of course, both ride horses; we cannot think of them without riding. They also live in the same time period, and they both feel themselves to be North Americans. However, as we said, in many other ways, they are different.

These two unlike archetypes are easily recognizable, even physically. We have already described the first one. The second one is showier and more sophisticated; he usually wears a fine mustache and dresses as an old Latin caballero, with dark hair and dark eyes, and his favorite weapon is not the gun but the foil. He prefers to fight with a foil, as the old knights did with a sword. This is a very significant symbol that will be analyzed later.

Whips are also used by both kinds of heroes, but while they are optional and only infrequently used by the English-heritage ones, they are almost indispensable for the heroes of Spanish descent. In fact, we may state that Spanish-heritage heroes are very fond of whips. Both archetypes also use the lasso.

Another feature that separates the two archetypes is how they treat women. While the English-heritage heroes usually try to avoid women and only flirt with them when they are completely trapped by the charm, beauty, and personality of a woman whom they really wish they would not love, the Spanish-heritage heroes openly behave flirtatiously and arrogantly with women, enjoying the confusion that their daring attitude produces in the female characters who receive their attention. In this aspect, they remind us of Don Juan. In some films, the Cisco Kid tries, very promiscuously, to kiss or seduce every beautiful woman he finds in his way, even making a joke out of his lack of respect toward women.

Another difference between both types of heroes is that while the English-heritage types go on their own, very frequently alone, the Spanish-heritage ones usually have a sidekick, usually a funny character, as their counterpoint. A kind of Sancho Panza, who many times is actually called Sancho, as in the case of Cisco Kid, and who sometimes may even be a funny, overweight priest, as in the case of Zorro. This sidekick helps the hero in all his adventures, giving the effect of a knight—a caballero—with a squire, almost like Don Quixote and Sancho Panza, an idea deeply rooted within Spanish culture.

And this leads us to the next difference: the social class. While the English-heritage type is usually an ordinary man, a John Doe, the Spanish-heritage hero can belong to a rich family and is generally more refined than the people who surround him. In the case of Zorro, he belongs to a kind of aristocracy of the country, and though he hides his identity, the audience knows it. We also know his parents, his family, and many times all his noble ancestors.

The clothes are also different. While the English-heritage heroes wear jeans and dusty, ordinary clothes, the Spanish-heritage heroes dress in smart, clean, almost shining clothing, reminding one of the charro outfit. Nevertheless, both of them wear riding boots.

For both Spanish-heritage heroes and English-heritage ones, we find two additional archetypes: the proper hero and the rascal. We can see them very clearly in the two most popular Spanish-heritage heroes: Cisco Kid and Zorro. While Zorro is a brave and ethical hero, Cisco Kid is not. This distinction also exists within the English-heritage ones, for example Billy the Kid and Wyatt Earp.

Indeed, the Cisco Kid and Billy the Kid are more antiheroes than heroes. Cisco Kid appears in many films as a charismatic, womanizing, Latin bandit with little sense of honor. He is a thief and a killer—brave, irresistible, but abominable. Ethically, he has much more in common with Billy the Kid than with the other Spanish-heritage hero, Zorro.

So, we may conclude that Cisco Kid is as fascinating and dishonest as Billy the Kid, and Zorro is as honorable and brave as Wyatt Earp. It's an interesting coincidence that both antiheroes, the Spanish-heritage one and the English-heritage antihero, are called "Kids," as if storytellers would seek to excuse their dishonesty as being kids: immature rascals or naughty boys.

In this way, we see how we can find the hero and the antihero within both American epic hero archetypes, and therefore in the roots of the American Western.

Chapter 2

# Hispanic Roots
# of the Western

IN THE BEGINNING was the horse. One cannot even begin to imagine a Western movie without the horse; there is little argument there. The lone cowboy rides a horse, and horses draw the stagecoach; they are an essential ingredient for the Hollywood Western. One can safely say that there would be no Hollywood Western movies without the horse. And there would be no horse in the New World if it were not for the Spaniard.[1]

It was the Spanish explorers and conquistadores who brought the animal to the New World, where it was unknown. The horses that the Spanish brought were highly valued, a mixture of Barb, Arabian, and Andalusian blood. History books are replete with stories about the key role that the horse played in Cortez's conquest of Mexico. Both Indigenous accounts and those of their Spanish conquerors tell of the astonishment the natives expressed when first faced with a Spaniard riding on what they called "stags," as their only association of such a creature was with a deer.[2] When the Spaniards were captured and sacrificed, their heads mounted on pikes, their horses suffered a similar fate.

In *The Hands of Cantú,* Tom Lea's well-researched novel about the introduction of the horse to the New World, he follows the adventures of a young Spaniard who learns a core principle of the conquistadors: keep the horse out of the hands of the Indigenous people they are trying to subdue. From the onset of their *conquistas*, the Spaniards knew that once the natives were mounted, they would prove a dangerous threat. At first, in Mexico, it was illegal for an Indian to either own or ride a horse. And so it is in the Hollywood Western: the Indian on horseback is a threat to the settlers and other poachers coming to take their land. The source may be the Spaniards, but the Native Americans in both Mexico and what would become the United States made themselves masters of horsemanship.

The significance of the horse to the Hollywood Western is reinforced by the fact that horses often shared the popularity of their owners. In this instance the Spanish roots are again relevant, for in discussions of the genesis of the Western genre, Cervantes's *Don Quixote* is often referenced. Like the steed of the Western hero, Quixote's Rocinante plays an important role in the hero's adventure. Zorro's horse Tornado may be the first famous hero's steed. He was a key player in Zorro's ongoing story. As the actors that played Zorro changed, so the horse also altered. Originally it was a black steed named Tornado, but then, inexplicably, Zorro rode a white horse named Phantom. The horse rearing back with the rider astride is a trademark Zorro move from the Disney series, which was emulated in later Westerns. Many Spanish paintings and sculptures also embody this feature.

Roy Rogers' Trigger may be the most famous of all the Hollywood cowboys' horses, but the Lone Ranger's call of "Hi, ho, Silver" made Silver a household name. This call to his horse began and ended every episode in the saga of the masked rider and his sidekick Tonto. Among other horses that achieved fame on their own are Gene Autrey's Champion and Lash La Rue's Black Diamond. Tom Mix's horse Tony acquired the moniker "The Wonder Horse" for his ability to perform numerous tricks. Even sidekicks had famous horses, such as Smiley Burnette's horse Ring Eye, recognizable by that eponymous marking. Gabby Hayes rode three different horses, but though he was a famous sidekick, his horses did not achieve equal fame, which may be because Hayes was not much of a rider. Of course, Pancho's horse Loco was a parallel noble steed to the Cisco Kid's Diablo.

But the cowboy is not the only one to ride a horse in the Hollywood Western movie; it is just as likely that the Indian is shown as an equally adept horseman. The advent of the horse changed the way of life for many different tribes. As a plant grows and multiplies branches, its root system mirrors the breadth and height of that growth.

The Spanish legacy of the horse in the New World cannot be overemphasized. It may have been Frederic Remington who put it best when he wrote,

> "One thing is certain; of all the remnants the Spaniard
> has left to glorify his reign in America, there will be none
> more worthy than his horse. . . . The Spaniard's horses may
> be found today in countless thousands, from the city of
> Montezuma to the region of perpetual snow; they are grafted
> into our equine wealth and make an important impression
> on the horse of the country. . . . [They have] borne the Moor,
> the Spanish conqueror, the red Indian, the mountain-man,
> and the vaquero through all the glories of their careers." [3]

The Spanish roots of the horse are undeniable. Another key element of the Hollywood Western is the issue of language. Here again, the Spanish roots are evident. Since the part of the United States that is most often the site or setting for the Western movie was first explored and settled by Spanish conquistadores, place-names and activities reflect the language of the mother country. Some examples will suffice: a number of Western movies take place in locations where Spanish has become so anglicized that it is humorous to think of them by their original Spanish names. Amarillo, for example, which means yellow in Spanish, is the lo-cale for a number of movies. Wouldn't it sound odd if the cowboys said they were going to "Yellow"? Or how about Los Banos or Los Gatos—"the baths" or "the cats"? In *The Hollywood Posse*, Diana Cary, writing about the Western from the perspective of the riding extras, doubles, and stuntmen, acknowledges the His-panic roots on the first page, writing about the *vaqueros, ranche-ros*, and others who "had little cause to greet . . . *gringo* traders with warm *abrazos*." [4]

A number of writers have documented the "remarkable pliancy" of the Western, and our metaphor of the Hispanic roots is meant to embrace such pliancy. [5] A garden or forest develops from many seeds and roots, and so the multiplicity of forms and directions of Western movies has blossomed and sprung forth in many cultures and climates. Similarly, Neil Campbell's central metaphor for his study of Western movies is the rhizome. Although he uses the metaphor in *The Rhizomatic West* to argue for detaching the Western from its "isolation as purely American," our purpose in this book is to focus on a significant aspect of the genre, one that is embodied in its very name.[6] A "Western" is that because its basic setting is in the western part of that land that came to be the United States. However, that location was not always part of the country; it must be remembered that it was first a Spanish colony and then, after the Mexican Revolution, became part of Mexico. Hence comes our focus on the Hispanic roots of the Western.

Don Miguel de Cervantes created a number of archetypes in *Don Quixote* that other authors replicated innumerable times as different countries and generations appropriated them. For our purposes, besides the fact that the story is originally Spanish, there is also the pattern of the hero and his sidekick. In Quixote's case it is the loyal Sancho Panza. Sometimes the pattern is very loose, but sometimes, as in the case of the Cisco Kid, the allusion is marked, as his sidekick is actually named Sancho and has a bit of a *panza* (belly).

There have been a number of studies concerning the image of Hispanics or Latinos on television or in the movies. Certainly, there can be no argument that negative stereotypes and images are rife. Of course, the same can be said about a number of other ethnic or minority groups. What is relevant for our study, however, is that whatever other images of Hispanics have been present in Hollywood movies, to quote Luis Reyes and Peter Rubie, "Despite the overwhelmingly negative images and stereotypes presented by mainstream American media, two positive Hispanic American heroes have managed to make it into popular American culture—Zorro and the Cisco Kid."[7] And to further our development of the story of the Hispanic roots of the Hollywood Western, it is significant that these two heroes are pioneers in the development of the genre. Thus, our book contains a chapter on each.

Chapter 3

# Cisco Kid

THE CISCO KID got off to a good start in the pantheon of Hollywood Western heroes. It certainly foretold success when Warner Baxter won an Academy Award in 1929 for his portrayal of the Cisco Kid in the movie *In Old Arizona*. Thus, Cisco was positively established in the pantheon of Western protagonists. And while that is a good beginning, there were many controversial issues stimulated by the nature of the character. First, there is the issue of the name.

Two questions arise from the name itself: one from "Cisco" and the other one from "Kid." The results are paradoxical. According to *Wikipedia*, "No first name is given in the story."[1] The O. Henry text keeps a certain ambiguity on this issue, which supports the Wikipedia interpretation. If we consider Cisco to refer to the character's first name, for Spanish-speaking persons the interpretation is quite clear, as the first idea that comes to mind when someone is called Cisco is that his first name is Francisco. "Cisco" is a common short form of "Francisco." Men named Francisco may opt for being called "Fran," "Curro," "Cisco," "Paco," or even "Pancho" in America. Thus, whether it is adopted during a man's life or given to the character at his birth—which is another issue, as we will see later—his first name is "Cisco" from "Francisco." And for some American readers, it might also mean that he comes from San Francisco.

Also meaningful is the fact that the word *cisco*, as a common term, has the meaning in Spanish of "fuss." We may say "se armó un cisco tremendo," meaning "a big fuss was made" or "a ruckus broke out." According to the Real Academia Española, *cisco* colloquially means *bullicio*, *reyerta*, or *alboroto* (bustle, ruckus, fight, clash, racket, fuss, or disturbance).[2] All these meanings are dramatically consistent with the personality and exploits of Cisco Kid. It cannot be a coincidence that these meanings so perfectly suit the features that characterize him. So, we may conclude that his first name is Francisco and that it became Cisco as a nickname, with dramatic consistency between its meaning as a Spanish word and the nature of the character. His name thus suggests more of an antihero than a hero.

Second, it is interesting that the other part of the name of the Hispanic-heritage antihero is "Kid." This means that he is recognized as a "kid," which means he is not considered a grown man. Kids are usually under parental authority, and their mistakes or faults are often smaller than the adult ones, even before the law. Naming a hero "Kid" implies considering him not completely responsible for his actions. It bears a kind of an implicit social understanding, almost indulgency or even complicity.

It is a contradictory feeling, like the one parents have for their kids when they are bullies at school. Most parents do not like their child to behave wrongly, but, deeply in their hearts, they admire him or her, believing that their naughty kid is someone very special, an independent leader with a strong personality, no matter if he or she is unethical, abusive, and harmful. Something like that is associated with the idea of giving the nickname of "Kid" to a bandit, making him, though an adult, a kind of a spoiled and never-grown member of society who is easily forgiven.

### Cisco's Surname: Is the Cisco Kid of Hispanic Origin?

Here, an interesting problem presents itself. Contrary to what most people think, José Manuel Rodríguez Humanes and Manuel Barrero assert that O. Henry's Cisco Kid "no era de origen hispano" (was not of Hispanic origin).[3] Moreover, O. Henry writes literally in "The Caballero's Way": "This *hombre* they call the Kid—Goodall is his name."[4] This means that his name is an English surname, Goodall, and not a Spanish name such as Pérez, García, or Vargas.

This idea that Cisco Kid is not Hispanic is reinforced in the text when O. Henry writes that "[Cisco] killed six men in more or less fair scrimmages, [and] had murdered twice as many (mostly Mexicans)." Why would a Mexican enjoy killing "mostly Mexicans"?[5] Because he was not Mexican or Hispanic. This notion is also supported by another line of the text: "It had been one of the Kid's pastimes to shoot Mexicans 'to see them kick': if he demanded from them moribund Terpsichorean feats, simply that he might be entertained, what terrible and extreme penalties would be certain to follow should they anger him!"[6] So, we may conclude, based on O. Henry's quotations, that Cisco Kid's full name is Cisco Goodall, someone who enjoyed killing Mexicans in particular.

The name Cisco Goodall leads us to two possibilities:

a) His full name may be Francisco Goodall, and he adopted the short form "Cisco." If so, he was the son of a man of English heritage and, probably, of a woman of Spanish heritage, who gave her son a name from her culture, leaving him the surname of the father's family and the first name of his mother's family.

b) His full name may be Frank Goodall, coming from a family of fully English heritage. But, as he was living in the West, he was finally nicknamed the Spanish equivalent "Francisco" and eventually became "Cisco."

This last possibility is dramatically consistent with the fact that he enjoyed "killing Mexicans," as being a Mexican and enjoying killing Mexicans sounds incongruous, as if he would be a kind of a cannibal. It would be less unusual if he were not a Mexican or of Hispanic heritage.

Further, would a bandit use his real name to identify himself after his misdeeds? Probably not. So, if his real name was Frank, a way to try to elude the legal punishment would be to mask his own name, Frank, with the Spanish equivalent, Cisco. This would also be dramatically consistent with the portrait that O. Henry paints of Cisco Kid: a smart bandit able to design a sophisticated revenge and kill a woman without using his own hands, and therefore smart enough to design the scheme of changing his real name if needed to elude the legal punishment.

If there is something that is clear about Cisco, it is that he was not dull; he was able to rob, kill, seduce, laugh, and always manage to leave the crime scene without being captured, in both books and films.

In any case, whether the real answer is "a" or "b," we may state —
considering the given data—that O. Henry's Cisco Kid, at most, is
half-Hispanic. But this fact does not match the image of the popular
Cisco Kid we all know, who is considered Hispanic by everybody.

Why is the Cisco Kid considered Hispanic? Did he claim it? No;
nowhere does he say, "I am Mexican" or "I am Hispanic," or "My ancestors were Spanish" in O. Henry's "The Caballero's Way," which
originated the famous character. We all feel he is Hispanic, but to
be honest, we do not really *know* it.

This description of Cisco Kid contrasts directly with Emilio
García Riera's perception of him. After reviewing all the films
starring Cisco Kid in his book *México visto por el cine extranjero
(Mexico as Seen in Foreign Films)*, he portrays Cisco Kid as "el
buen bandido mexicano," which means "the good Mexican bandit."[7] That is quite a paradox: is it possible to be a bandit and to be
good? But this is another question that we will deal with later. In
the Wikipedia article on Cisco Kid, this contradiction is also pointed out: "In movies and television, the Kid was depicted as a heroic
Mexican caballero, even though he was originally a cruel outlaw."[8]

How did it happen? The literary character is a villain, but the
adaptation of this fictional figure that occurred in movies, in radio and television series, and in comic books is quite a different
one: someone funny, seductive, and loved by the audience for many,
many years, even as late as 1994, when the last TV movie about
the Kid was shot. All this means that the literary figure and the cinematographic one are very different, probably even physically, and
that there is disagreement both about his cultural origin and about
his personality and aspect.

Strictly speaking, what really makes us believe that he is Hispanic is what in legal terminology is called "circumstantial evidence,"
as we will see.

In "The Caballero's Way," it happens because of the word
"caballero," understanding that if he was a caballero, he was
Hispanic. But again, in O. Henry's text, the Kid never says of himself that he was a caballero; the exact quotation in question is, "He
was muy caballero, as the Mexicans express it, where the ladies
were concerned."[9] This clearly means either that the Mexicans

considered Cisco Kid a caballero, or that he was a gentleman with women, and that the Mexicans express this with the word "caballero," suitable for Cisco Kid but nothing else. And though the word "caballero" is Spanish, it can be applied to anyone—British, French, Italians, etc.—if they behave like caballeros.

Additionally, the fact that his lover was called Tonia does not make Cisco himself Hispanic. O. Henry described Tonia as "a half-Mexican girl," and she may have been a woman who was going out with two men who were antagonistic to each other: Lieutenant Sandridge and Goodall, who was a bandit known by the nickname "Cisco Kid."[10] If neither of these men were of Hispanic heritage, it would not have been a confrontation between a Hispanic and a Caucasian but a fight between a law man and an outlaw. And if so, O. Henry's story would not be satirical through the use of Hispanic men (calling themselves "caballeros" while coldly killing the women who betray them), but satirical through cynical so-called caballeros doing so, wherever they may come from, no matter if they are of Spanish or English heritage.

In films, we feel that Cisco Kid is Hispanic because of his clothes and other features, though we will see how these features are not exclusively Hispanic. For instance, his peculiar mustache could be identified by some people as "Hispanic," but it is also like Errol Flynn's. The fact that Cisco Kid says some words in Spanish is not determinant either, as many English-speaking people use occasional Spanish words in the United States without being of Hispanic heritage.

Other apparent pieces of evidence in specific films are also questionable. One present in the film *In Old Arizona* is when Cisco Kid says his whole name when introducing himself to Sergeant Mickey Dunn (something that is a complete invention with regard to the story, as O. Henry never mentioned such a name in "The Caballero's Way"). Cisco says, "My name is Conrado Sebastián Rodrigo Don Juan Chicuello," which is a funny combination.[11] If this were a real person's name, it would mean that he has four names and one surname. His use of the word "don" is also bizarre, as he includes "Don Juan" in the middle of all the other names! In Spanish if you say *don*, you use it at the beginning of the name as a title of respect. In this way, he should have said, "Don Conrado Sebastián Rodrigo Juan." Why does he instead say "Don Juan" after "Conrado Sebastián Rodrigo"? He gives all these weird names in a bizarre way, as well, in a scene where he was teasing Sergeant Dunn, as he knew that Sergeant Dunn was trying to capture Cisco Kid without knowing that the Kid was next to him. So, Cisco Kid may be pulling his leg in two ways: being next to him and telling him a string of false Spanish names. Moreover, he says to Tonia, when he is declaring his love to her, that he comes from Portugal, where he ran away from his parents when he was a kid, and that he wants to go back there with her to start a new life. But if he is Portuguese, he should have had Portuguese names, which reinforces the idea that all these given Spanish names are a lie invented for the Sergeant.

Another question is whether his aspect is that of a man who could be both Hispanic and Caucasian. This is obvious by the fact that Warner Baxter, who played the Cisco Kid in 1928 in *In Old Arizona*, also played Jay Gatsby in *The Great Gatsby* in 1926. Moreover, the actor who was initially scheduled to be the Cisco Kid was Raoul Walsh, who was going to star in and direct the film until an accident in which he lost his eye. Neither Baxter nor Walsh were Hispanic.

Nevertheless, despite all this data, what we all feel is that Cisco Kid is Hispanic.

But what is more important for a fictional character, the idea the author has of the character (expressed with words and images in both the text and the film) or the idea the audience has of the character after knowing him or her? There are many compelling theories on both the author's and the audience's responses, but nowadays most critics support respecting the audience's understanding of the works, regardless of the author's intentions when creating them. So, we may conclude by stating that if we all *feel* that Cisco Kid is Hispanic, he is so.

Nevertheless, for those who may feel disquieted or disappointed about the doubts we've generated regarding Cisco's Hispanic heritage, we may suggest considering the following reasoning. First, if he is an English-heritage character, it means that this rascal that everybody thought was Hispanic is probably a Caucasian pretending to look Hispanic, through his nickname "Cisco," as a way to mask his own identity. Second, this cinematographic, nice, and funny version of Cisco Kid is still a robber, a murderer, and a male chauvinist, always cheating and fooling women. Who wants to be part of his group anyway? So, the conclusion may be that if he is Caucasian, it is not such bad news for Hispanic culture!

In contrast, Zorro is a real caballero, and he truly loves his lover—only one woman—and he only steals and kills for justice or to help the poor. In short, he is a real Robin Hood. The Cisco Kid, on the other hand, only resembles Robin Hood in some later movies where the character was highly distorted and really only a naïve, standard caricature. About these last films and the strips that later appeared in newspapers and comics, Diego Cordoba described the character with these words: "[It] was supposedly based on a O. Henry story, but in fact, had very little to do with it (it looked more like a Lone Ranger without the mask and with a Mexican friend instead of a Native American one)."[12]

The original Cisco Kid feels pleasure killing (particularly Mexicans) and steals for himself and does not truly love any woman. Even Tonia, the beloved of the Kid in "The Caballero's Way" and in the film *In Old Arizona*, was not really loved. (Or is there still nowadays anyone gullible enough to believe that a person who is able to coldly kill his or her lover actually loves him or her?)

O. Henry, already in 1907, made it clear: Cisco Kid was an unpleasant and simple villain whose pride was wounded by his lover, and because of that he wanted to kill her, but without touching her, because his idea of being a caballero did not allow him to be rude to a woman. For Cisco Kid, being a caballero had nothing to do with being noble or honorable, or loving and respectful, or at least nice. Rather, his idea of being a caballero only meant to have "gentle words [with women, as he] . . . knew how to treat a lady."[13] He did, indeed, know how to treat her: killing her for not loving him and for betraying him, but, of course, doing it without touching her, as is the caballero's way!

O. Henry does not leave any loose ends in his short story, as the elaborate critique he makes of Cisco Kid—ridiculing not only him but also those who admire him in his world and satirizing the society to which he belongs—is pointed out within both cultural spheres, the Hispanic and the English. To the Hispanic, O. Henry points out this misconception of what "being a caballero" means, and to the English, he names the Kid (certainly ironically), Goodall.

To conclude, all the clues, both in English and Spanish, lead us to realize sarcastically that Cisco Kid was neither "all good" nor a caballero. Nevertheless, the complete answer to the question, "Is Cisco Kid really a Hispanic Western hero?" will be given after reviewing all the angles of this issue, and we need to go deeper within this character and its meaning to give an answer.

### The Big Unknown in Europe in Films, TV, and Radio Series

Cisco Kid is very well known in the United States and in Mexico, but practically unknown in Spain and most of the rest of Europe. Why is that?

There are many reasons. The main one probably is because Cisco Kid was portrayed not only in films but also, and mainly, in many radio and television series in the United States throughout the twentieth century. These TV series were not sold to Europe, so nobody saw Cisco Kid on TV in Spain, France, Germany, Italy, etc. This fact, undoubtedly, cut the possibility of its diffusion through the most significant media, the television. *The Lone Ranger*, *Bonanza*, and *Little House on the Prairie* were all watched in many European homes, but Cisco Kid was not.

The second reason is that the same thing happened with the radio series: while in the United States Cisco Kid appeared on the radio in a weekly series from 1942 until 1945, followed by a thrice weekly series in 1946, and then in a series of more than six hundred episodes from 1947 to 1956, in Spain and the other European countries he did not appear in any episode.[14]

The tone of this "radio-Cisco Kid" in the United States certainly helped him to increase his popularity. He was fun and nice: the radio episodes ended with Cisco or Pancho—his faithful servant and friend—making a joke about the adventure they had completed, laughing and saying, "Oh, Pancho!" or "Oh, Cisco!" before galloping off to end the episode. He was a fellow everybody liked and a character to be remembered.

The third reason has been the fact that O. Henry has never been a popular writer in Europe.

Finally, the fourth reason is probably connected with the features of the character of Cisco Kid. Though the version of Cisco Kid portrayed on radio and television had little to do with the original Cisco Kid—being much kinder and nicer than O. Henry's original version—Cisco was still always touching the limits of what was tolerable: with women, with poor people, and with everybody. He was not only an outlaw but also a rascal with no ethics and no principles. This personality made him a difficult hero to export. His questionable behavior made him a controversial figure who was many times not suitable for children. And, on the other hand, he and his stories were too naïve for adults.

Some people may think that his local nature might also have influenced his lack of popularity in Europe, but this idea is contradicted by the fact that Zorro, another "local" American hero, is very well known in Europe and in most places of the world.

Zorro is a universal character known by, we may say, everybody in the Western world. Zorro is part of our collective imaginary, to use Edgar Morin's concept.[15] He is in our heads and hearts, as meaningful as Superman, Lewis Carroll's Alice, Herman Melville's Moby Dick, or Walt Disney's Mickey Mouse: a fictional figure that is part of our lives whether we like it or not. In short, Zorro is a hero, a modern William Tell. And he has survived the test of time, starring in big films even in the twenty-first century.

Moreover, Zorro has crossed borders between countries and continents not only because of its multicultural audience but probably also because of the European actors who have starred as Don Diego de la Vega. Two very popular and seductive modern European actors have played the role of Zorro: a French actor, Alain Delon, in the film *Zorro* (1974), and a Spanish one, Antonio Banderas, in *The Mask of Zorro* (1998) and *The Legend of Zorro* (2005). These actors made Zorro a very relevant and updated reference for European audiences. Zorro was already famous, but watching him played by Delon and Banderas was seeing Zorro as part of European culture, propitiating a certain kind of cultural appropriation and identification of the audience, in both America and Europe.

In conclusion, Zorro has become a universal hero, while Cisco Kid is a local antihero.


## Technology, Coincidence, and Success

Considering Cisco Kid a big success within American movies and television without paying attention to two coincidental technical circumstances would not be fair.

It happens that the feature film that was nominated for five Academy Awards, including Best Picture, and which won the Best Actor Award in 1929, *In Old Arizona*, was a major innovation in Hollywood. It was the first major Western to use the technology of sound and the first talkie to be shot outdoors on authentic, beautiful American locations in California and Utah. We can imagine the impact that sound and the authentic outdoors made on the audience and the critics. This does not mean that the film did not deserve the audience attention and the awards it received, but certainly this technical novelty was a great plus for the film; it could have been a story about Cisco Kid, Al Capone, or the Wizard of Oz. *In Old Arizona* (1928) was directed by Raoul Walsh and Irving Cummings, two masters of universal cinema.

Similar fortune was had by the television series *The Cisco Kid,* broadcast between 1950 and 1956, as it happens to be that it was the first TV series filmed in color. It is not difficult to consider how the color TV impacted the spectators. Again, the issue is beyond whether the story was about Cisco Kid or someone else. The character of Cisco Kid had the advantage of being coincidentally released at the same time that a technical novelty was introduced to the audiences for the first time. This is something that undoubtedly on both historical occasions—for both feature film lovers and TV lovers—increased his popularity.

## Cisco Kid in Feature Films

Cisco Kid's initial success is, undoubtedly, linked to feature films. And though many films have been made about this character, the most remarkable movie based on him was the one released in 1928, the already mentioned and multi-awarded *In Old Arizona*. It was not the first film based upon this character, however. Webster Cullison directed the first movie about Cisco Kid in 1914, played by William R. Dunn. Currently, there is not even a single picture of this actor, so we cannot know what this first human image of the Kid was like. We only know that it was a short movie, silent and in black and white, titled *The Caballero's Way*. In 1919, a second film on Cisco Kid was released. The actor who played Cisco Kid was Vester Pegg, and the film was called *The Border Terror*. Up to today, there are no images of this film.

With the lack of information about these two films, it is fair to say that the oldest existing film about Cisco Kid is *In Old Arizona* (1928). And as we will see, it is not only the oldest but also the best one.

As we mentioned, the fact that it was also the first Western talkie and, moreover, the first film shot outdoors, portraying beautiful landscapes in California and Utah, made it a very special and important movie, beyond its own merits. The fact that it was going to be starred in and directed by Raoul Walsh was also meaningful in itself regarding its eventual transcendence and the importance that its producers gave to the story.

It is a pity that a hare jumped through the windshield of a car when Walsh was driving, injuring him in the eye and not allowing him to continue acting in the film. Walsh needed help to continue directing the movie, so Irving Cummings was called to help him, and both appeared in the credits of the film as co-directors. Nevertheless, even though Raoul Walsh needed help to finish the film, we can feel his masterful style and his narrative pulse, making it a memorable film. It thoroughly deserved the award and the five nominations it received at the academy.

The actor who played Cisco Kid, replacing Walsh, was Warner Baxter, who not only got the Academy Award for Best Actor in 1929 but also became "the Cisco Kid" *par excellence*, starring in four more films: *The Arizona Kid* (1930), co-starring Carole Lombard; *The Cisco Kid* (1931); and *The Stolen Jools* (1931), a film where many Hollywood actors appeared in cameos in order to raise funds for the National Vaudeville Artists Tuberculosis Sanitarium. In *The Cisco Kid*, Warner Baxter appeared together with Buster Keaton, Edward G. Robinson, Gary Cooper, and Joan Crawford, which gives us the measure of the importance of this Spanish-heritage antihero at that time. Lastly, he starred in *The Return of the Cisco Kid* (1939).

In this last film, while Baxter played the Cisco Kid, a younger actor played a minor role (López). His name was Cesar Romero. Baxter did not know that Romero was the one who was going to replace him playing Cisco Kid in the next six feature films: *The Cisco Kid and the Lady* (1939); *Lucky Cisco Kid* (1940), with Dana Andrews as Sergeant Dunn; *Viva Cisco Kid* (1940); *The Gay Caballero* (1940); *Romance of the Rio Grande* (1940); and *Ride on Vaquero* (1941). During the next four years, there were no films produced about Cisco Kid. Having shot four films about him in 1940 probably saturated the audience.

But in 1945 he returned powerfully. In 1945 three films about the Kid were shot, all of them starring Duncan Renaldo: *The Cisco Kid Returns*, *In Old New Mexico*, and *South of Rio Grande*. Unexpectedly, Renaldo was replaced in 1946 by Gilbert Roland, who played the Kid in three feature films that year: *The Gay Cavalier*, *South of Monterey*, and *Beauty and the Bandit*. In 1947 he made two more movies about the Kid: *Riding the California Trail* and *Robin Hood of Monterey*, when, suddenly, he was replaced by the one who substituted him two years earlier—Duncan Renaldo. Roland's attempt to be Cisco Kid barely lasted a couple of years!

With Duncan Renaldo back again playing the Cisco Kid, the character little by little faded. He starred in five more films as the Cisco Kid: *The Valiant Hombre* (1948), *The Gay Amigo* (1949), *The Daring Caballero* (1949), *Satan's Cradle* (1949), and *The Girl from San Lorenzo* (1950).

The first half of the twentieth century had been full of stories about and actors playing Cisco Kid, but, suddenly, in the second half, there was a big silence. No more stories or feature films were shot based on this character, except for one: the TV movie *The Cisco Kid* (1994), starring Jimmy Smits and directed by Luis Valdez, which lasted ninety-one minutes and was made for the TNT Network.

Twenty-seven films on Cisco Kid were shot before 1950, and only one after 1950. How did it happen that such a popular character became practically "nothing" within the feature film industry?

Several reasons can explain this result. First of all, fortunately or unfortunately, it happened that the best of all these films was the first existing one: *In Old Arizona*. From that powerful start, having achieved such a level, the most likely evolution was going to go down from the summit to the end, falling slowly step by step.

No film based on Cisco Kid can be compared with *In Old Arizona*. It not only inspired the passion of all the audiences, the critics, and the academy but also became a great economic success, not reached by any of the following movies. Its box office revenue reached $1.3 million, which makes this movie clearly a bestseller.[16] And nowadays, it is still well-known and enjoys the reputation of a classic.

Second, in the 1950's, after World War II, everything changed, and a character like Cisco Kid became "old." As a matter of fact, when he returned in 1994, all the publicity focused on the fact that it was "the return of a legend."

Moreover, all these films evolved in a natural way to other formats: (1) from 1942 to 1956 on the radio; (2) from 1950 to1956 on TV, where 156 episodes were broadcast; and (3) from 1944 to 2009 on strips in newspapers, comics, and graphic novels.

### The Men Who Embodied Cisco Kid, Their Films, and the Academy Awards

It is curious how most actors who played the role of Cisco Kid were not Hispanic. If we see the faces of all those actors in Wikipedia, or on the film posters printed when the Cisco Kid films were released, we may be surprised as the actors are characterized as Hispanic without being it until the 1940's, when we finally find the first Hispanic actor playing Cisco Kid: Cesar Romero.

These different films about Cisco Kid that were shot throughout the twentieth century, and the posters designed for their promotion, will also allow us to perceive the aesthetic evolution of the myth and the type of films they were. It is also interesting to see the actresses who are portrayed on the film posters, as there has been a noticeable change in the type of woman who is Cisco Kid's partner as the years have passed by. Lastly, the evolution of the film titles is revelatory, too, of a change in the social perception of the character.

To go deeper into these questions, it is necessary to watch the films in chronological order, and to investigate, at least in Wikipedia, the professional trajectory of the main actors and directors who made those films.

William R. Dunn was the first actor who played the role of Cisco Kid in films. The movie was shot in 1914 and titled *The Caballero's Way*. This first film shot about Cisco Kid has been lost, and so far—unless future findings may help it—not even an image of it has been saved. To this we must add there are no known photographs of William R. Dunn. But just considering his name we can conclude that he was not Hispanic. The only extant document relating to this film is a picture of it published on the internet, where it is said that the whole film crew appears. As far as we know, the film plot was very similar to O. Henry's story, and both had the same title, "The Caballero's Way."

Vester Pegg was the second actor who played Cisco Kid. He starred as Cisco in the film *The Border Terror* (1919). Again, there are no images of this movie, though perhaps one day in the future a copy of it may appear; at least until now and with the available data, it seems that it has also been lost. In any case, the film title is explicit by itself of the treatment that the character of Cisco Kid received in this second film on him: "The Border *Terror*." We can imagine Cisco Kid being feared by everyone living or wandering around the frontier. People were frightened and felt "terror" just hearing his name. Fortunately, there are some pictures of Vester Pegg in other films, as he made many Westerns. We can see his face in many different pictures dressed as a cowboy and can clearly see that he, too, was not a Hispanic man. He was born in Appleton City, Missouri. We can catch a glimpse of Vester Pegg's acting in the silent Western *Bare Firsts* (1919), directed by John Ford (available on the internet).

In 1928, the actor who played Cisco Kid was Warner Baxter, in the film *In Old Arizona*. This is the already-mentioned film that in 1929 was multi-awarded: nominated for five Academy Awards, including Best Picture, and winner of the Best Actor Award.

These recognitions mean, in a certain way, a triple honor. First, winning any Oscar is an honor in itself. Second, this also means that the second Best Actor Academy Award in the history of cinema was given to an actor playing a Hispanic hero/antihero: Cisco Kid. Third, the first Western to receive an award from the Academy starred a Hispanic character belonging to Hispanic culture. These Hispanic Hollywood Western roots are indeed honorable, deep, and meaningful.

This success pushed Warner Baxter to play Cisco Kid in many different films until 1939. But, of course, as all his predecessors, though he was playing a Hispanic character, he was not Hispanic.

In 1939, another actor, Cesar Romero, substituted him playing the Cisco Kid role in feature films. Romero played Cisco Kid from 1939 to 1941. For the first time, the actor playing Cisco Kid was an American of Hispanic heritage, born in New York City in 1907. His mother was from Cuba, and his father from Spain.

During the first half of the twentieth century, many films were shot with Cisco Kid as the protagonist. In 1945, Duncan Renaldo replaced Cesar Romero, starting what we may call his first period as Cisco Kid, because soon, in 1946, another actor, Gilbert Roland, played Cisco Kid, too, in another feature film. Roland shot several films as this character over a period of two years, but in 1948, Duncan Renaldo returned to the screen again as Cisco Kid for several more years, starting his second period as Cisco Kid in movies.

During the second half of the twentieth century, the film audience's passion for Cisco Kid decreased, but it did not completely disappear, as we even find a film on Cisco Kid in 1994 played by the actor Jimmy Smits. The title of the film, characteristically, is *The Cisco Kid*.

## Cisco Kid in Spanish and American Comics and Strips

In the United States, the first comic adaptation appeared in 1944. It was a comic book based on the radio series and titled *Cisco Kid Comics* and published by Baily Publishing in one volume. Later, from 1950 to 1958, Dell Comics published a series of forty-one comics written and drawn by different authors. This series was named *The Cisco Kid*.

After the success of the TV series, King Featured Syndicated (KFS) provided a new format for Cisco Kid, beginning on January 15, 1951: the newspaper strip. Cisco Kid appeared in more than three hundred newspapers in America in a comic strip drawn by the Argentinian José Luis Salinas and written by Rod Reed. It was published in Argentina, too, in the newspaper *La Razón* and in the magazine *Patoruzito*. These strips lasted until August 10, 1968. The strip ran for almost eighteen years.

In all these comics and strips, Cisco Kid appeared as a Mexican caballero defending the poor and fighting the crime and corruption that were rampant in New Mexico at the end of the nineteenth century. This Cisco Kid, who appeared in strips and comics, was closer to the Lone Ranger than to himself at his origin. He was not a sadist bandit but an adventurer stealing from the rich and corrupt to help the poor and honest. The legend says that people at King Features, though gladly surprised by the results, asked Salinas if it were possible to make the character a little more manly.

The Cisco Kid strip ended as only a daily and never got a Sunday page, which has been considered by many comic lovers as unfair, for if there were any strip that could hold up to Foster's Prince Valiant, it was Salina's Cisco Kid.

After a long silence, Cisco Kid reappeared again in some graphic novels published by Moonstone Books (2004–2009): *The Cisco Kid: Hell's Gate*, *The Cisco Kid vs. Wyatt Earp*, *The Cisco Kid: Gunfire and Brimstone*, and *The Cisco Kid*.

In Spain, the American comic strip about Cisco Kid, from the years 1951 to 1953, was bought and published in Spanish in 1989 as *Cisco Kid*. The series was part of a comic collection named "Héroes de siempre" in art comics. The collection was cancelled after the seventh issue, as KFS could not provide the original material for its reproduction. The comic did not have much relevance.

With regard to the strips in Spain, in 1950 a Spanish magazine—devoted to kids and called *Chicos*—included a Cisco Kid strip, but it did not become popular. A second attempt was made between 1955 and 1958 by two local newspapers, *Madrid* and *Levante*, but once again with little success. The third time that Cisco Kid tried to conquer Spain was in 1974. Grafimart Ediciones published two *tebeos* (comics for children) starring Cisco Kid, and in 1975 six more. Juan Marti Pavón was the editor, and the comics were published under the name "Chito Extraordinario." This is probably the most successful of all the Cisco Kid incursions into Spanish kids' world. The fourth and final attempt was made by Ediciones Vértice in 1980, publishing twenty-two numbers of the adventures of Cisco Kid. All these publishing efforts were remarkable, but with very little success.

We may conclude that while Cisco Kid was very well-known among most people in America, in Europe (including Spain), practically nobody knows him (with the possible exception of a comic/*tebeo* enthusiast).

### Nash Candelaria: Closing O. Henry's Literary Circle on Cisco Kid

It is remarkable how, when his films, series, strips, and comics were fading in significance, Cisco Kid found a new way of having a presence within the American cultural landscape: in books again, thus closing the circle started by O. Henry almost a hundred years ago.

The book that closes O. Henry's circle around Cisco Kid is a collection of short stories written by the Mexican-American novelist Nash Candelaria in 1988, where a short story, "The Day Cisco Kid Shot John Wayne," uses the title to link this Hispanic-heritage antihero with the English-heritage hero *par excellence*, John Wayne. The author, Candelaria, throws a wink to the whole story of Westerns. When he published this story, he had already won the American Book Award in 1983 for his work *Not by the Sword,* and he also had been Finalist at the Western Writers of America Awards for two works in different categories: Best Western Historical Novel and Best Western Short Fiction.

Moreover, Cisco Kid and even Pancho eventually have also reappeared within some lines of dialogue and as characters' nicknames in Stephen King short stories and in their film adaptations. This is most notable in "The Raft," a horror short story published in the 1986 collection *Skeleton Crew*, and again in a 2007 collection, *Everything's Eventual: 14 Dark Tales*, where King writes, "The lady doc, Ms. Cisco Kid, hadn't even *looked* at me . . ."[17]

Stephen King has not been the only one to use Cisco and Pancho's names within his fiction. "Characters who use 'Cisco' and 'Pancho' as nicknames can be found in . . . Michael Connelly's novels *The Brass Verdict* (2008) and *The Fifth Witness* (2011)."[18] In these novels a character called Dennis "Cisco" Wojciechowski appears. He is a private investigator who works for the main character of the series, Mickey Haller, and is formerly associated with a Road Saints motorcycle gang who bestowed him with the nickname Cisco in reference to Cisco Kid.

We also find allusions to Cisco Kid in movies such as *Stand by Me* (1986), directed by Rob Reiner and based on a Stephen King story; *Wild at Heart* (1990), directed by David Lynch and based on a novel written by Barry Gifford, where Nicolas Cage plays the role of "a kind of a romantic Southern outlaw";[19] and *Creepshow 2* (1987), directed by Michael Gornick and also based on three Stephen King stories. Lastly, some TV series feature allusions to Cisco Kid, as in *Hill Street Blues* and *CSI: Crime Scene Investigation*.[20]

All these allusions are subtle nods from the members of society who find in Cisco Kid, after around a century, a reference that is relevant to them, no matter if the members are rich or poor, Hispanic or English, men or women: these artists, filmmakers, writers, and their readers and audiences know who Cisco Kid is and what he means, showing us how alive he still is within our minds and hearts, something that is a real and meaningful accomplishment.

**Cisco Kid and the Music: O. Henry and *In Old Arizona* (1928)**

One of the narrative achievements of both the written story "The Caballero's Way" and the award-winning film *In Old Arizona* is the music. In the book, Cisco Kid sings when he rides on his horse from one place to another: "He had a voice like a coyote with bronchitis, but whenever he chose to sing his song he sang it."[21] In the film, Cisco Kid not only sings but also listens to the gramophone when visiting his girlfriend, listening to the beautiful song "My Tonia," composed for the film by B. G. De Sylva, Lew Brown (music), and Ray Henderson (lyrics), and recorded for the first time in December 1928.

Within O. Henry's short story, when Cisco rides his horse and feels like it, he obsessively sings the following lines:

> *Don't you monkey with my Lulu girl*
> *Or I'll tell you what I'll do—*[22]

This little song is an encapsulation of the story. It floats in the air as a portentous menace, poetically creating a certain type of suspense that finally floods the story. As a matter of fact, it becomes the spirit of the tsunami that ends Tonia's life and is so meaningful that these words are also the last ones in O. Henry's story.

In the film *In Old Arizona*, the equivalent to this song is:

> *I'll send my gal to the city*
> *And I send my gal to the town . . .*
> *And my gel, she's young . . . and she's pretty*
> *And she's ready to settle down*[23]

Warner Baxter sings this song several times throughout the movie, beginning when he has stolen money from a stagecoach and decides to visit his girlfriend. It is the first time he mentions her, and in a good mood he starts singing while riding. He only sings the two first lines and leaves the song hanging in the air. Then, after having been shaved at the barbershop, he sings it again, feeling well seeing his face clean and introducing part of the third line. At this point, the sergeant knocks at the barbershop door, and they meet. And later, when the barber and the sergeant are talking about finding and killing the Cisco Kid, and he is having a bath in the room next to them, hearing them, and laughing at their words, Cisco sings it once more, this time introducing the fourth and last line, smiling happily. The song is perfectly integrated within the drama, unveiling who they are and what they want. Again, like in O. Henry's story, the song creates suspense and carries a menace for all the protagonists of the story.

While Cisco sings to his beloved one, the sergeant sings as well, but he sings no words, just a tune that he puts to these sounds: "Ta-ra-ra bom-di-ay . . . ," something that he happily repeats many times. He sings when he is presented for the first time in the plot while playing with other soldiers, when he is waiting to be shaved, etc. But while Cisco sings clear words, he says nothing intelligible, only "Ta-ra-ra bom-bom-di-di-ay . . . ," perhaps introducing some variations but always saying nothing.[24] But both sing happily and express their security in themselves through their singing. It is like a soft and mellifluous tone that is yet warlike, ironically and humorously challenging each other.

The Cisco Kid gives us the impression that he is considering marrying Tonia or otherwise linking his life to her and living together, as he emphasizes the fact that she is "ready to settle down" in his song. This is an idea that is later confirmed when he proposes to her that they leave the United States to go back to his childhood land, Portugal. But we as the audience know much more than he knows. From an omniscient point of view—as the story is told to us—we can see in the film how during the first visit Cisco pays to Tonia, she is with another man in her room, and how, when she knows the Kid is arriving, she encourages the man to run away and hide from Cisco. She appears as a young woman who receives older men, getting presents and money from them after they enjoy her sexual favors.

We pity Cisco and his candor and passion for his Tonia, whom he considers to be an angel—he tells her outright, "You are an angel"—when we know that she is closer to the devil. She later flirts with the sergeant, and after having had sex with him, she even asks him if there are more handsome soldiers like him in the camp. This question really surprises the sergeant: he is shocked to find a teen-ager who is betraying Cisco by being with him and who is, at the same time, wondering if there are other handsome fellows to flirt with right around the corner. She looks even more flirtatious than Prosper Merimée's Carmen, something that reminds us of the description O. Henry gives of her in the original story: "half Carmen, half Madonna."[25]

As the film goes on, the little song grows, and Cisco finishes it with another line:

*I'll send my gal to the city*
*And I send my gal to the town . . .*
*And my gel, she's young . . . and she's pretty*
*Her flirting days are over*
*And she's ready to settle down*[26]

He still sings it happily, however, as if a teenager who has been a flirt in her youth would be ready to settle, join her man, and grow a family. Cisco seems to believe that he was going to be this man who gives a reason for her flirting—as a search for a partner—because the time for "settling" has arrived and he is offering her the supposedly desired "settling down."

But Cisco does not know that she is ambitious and that she does not really care for that "settling," nor for love. She only cares for money, clothes, hats, and going to New York, where better shops can be found. When she hears his proposal to go to Portugal, she looks at him in astonishment. How can he wish to make such a proposal?

As the plot is being developed, the song gets another meaning each time he sings it. Finally, it means that her flirting times are over because she is going to die, and the "settling" is her grave. This is similar to O. Henry's story, which ended with Cisco Kid singing sinisterly:

*Don't you monkey with my Lulu girl*
*Or I'll tell you what I'll do—*[27]

*In Old Arizona* ends with Warner Baxter singing:

> *Her flirting days are over*
> *And she's ready to settle down*

Both the book and the film are great: two masterpieces. All these subtle, well-done, and consistent dramatic proposals are wonderful, and, moreover, they are not the only ones in the film. We also find the fine and rigorous use of the gramophone playing the song "My Tonia" each time Cisco arrives at Tonia's home or when she is with a man there, and we even hear Baxter singing the song to "his Tonia" while playing a guitar. All these actions are as dance, where all the actions flow to the next one with perfect serenity, but increasing the dramatic tension, and coldly and intensely precipitating the tragedy. As Bruce F. Kawin remarked on Howard Hawks's filmmaking: "The most accomplished characteristic of Hawks's films is their rhythm. . . . It is not just a question of the meter and pace of dialogue, but of the way dialogue, music, camera, position, and actor movement are gracefully coordinated."[28] It has the mastery of Ford's and Shakespeare's tragedies, where in a calm and humorous way we go forward to the inescapable ending.

And, last but not least, the use of musical bands throughout the film is remarkable. Suddenly, in the middle of the street appears a group of musicians, including a violin player. We know that they are all Mexicans because of their clothes, and it appears to be something "natural" within village life, just as we find people selling fruit or waiting for the stagecoach. Similarly, we later see some soldiers waiting for the stagecoach and beautifully singing a cappella. Or the sergeant's mates, having fun playing the harmonica in the evening next to the river.

Every piece of music is part of the story, and enriches it, giving the film the strength of an opera. In fact, *In Old Arizona* starts and ends—as was usual for silent movies—with an overture played by an orchestra, in this case playing "My Tonia." It is seductive, moving, and impressive. It has the flavor of a Mozart's opera.

Undoubtedly, this film is a masterpiece that has been largely neglected so far and has not been studied as it should have been. There is mastery and finesse in the use of music, consistently integrated, offering us an outstanding paradigm. Additionally, it is both a classical and avant-garde film even nowadays. It connects fully with the influential movement that appeared at the end of the twentieth century, Dogme 95. With *In Old Arizona,* we find a film shot at the beginning of the twentieth century fulfilling the rules of this innovative movement of the beginning of the twenty-first century. This cinema movement is such a novel phenomenon for filmmaking, a century after the creation of cinema, that it is surprising to see how a film shot in 1928 follows Dogme 95 Manifesto rules so literally.

This avant-garde filmmaking movement, started by the Danish directors Lars von Trier and Thomas Vinterberg, states in its manifesto that "The sound must never be produced apart from the images or *vice versa.* (Music must not be used unless it occurs where the scene is being shot.)"[29] Never has a film followed this rule so naturally.

We are not surprised that the Academy and the audience were overwhelmed with *In Old Arizona*, transforming Cisco Kid definitively into a mythical character.

### Deep Purple, Elvis Presley, Many Others, and Cisco Kid

Cisco Kid and his faithful friend Pancho have been so significant in American culture and identity that they appear and reappear in the most unexpected ways. For example, we find a song composed by the English hard rock band Deep Purple in their album *Purpendicular* (1996) titled "Hey Cisco," where both Cisco and Pancho are remembered with certain melancholy. The group offers a kind of ode to friendship and to Cisco's style, with his hat, his gun, and his half cigarette. They portray Cisco as a legendary rider heading off into the sunset:

*Watch him ride into the sunset*
*He'd have the little fat guy*
*Right along his side*
*Echoing off the canyon, Hey Cisco*
*From Pancho 'n' pretty soon*

*The black sombrero would reply*
*[ . . . ]*

*Can't open no more supermarkets*
*Duncan's sombrero's hanging*
*Up there with his guns*
*Some cigarro sucking slag*
*Under a chip Hollywood chandelier*
*Says 'Cisco, Kid you know*
*Your day is done*
*Let me know how you are doin'*
*Mr Renaldo*
*If you need me I could be*
*A friend for life*
*[ . . . ]*

*I'll stay to the end*
*Hey Cisco*
*Let's go out in style*
*We're going down together*[30]

Cisco Kid's image is so powerful that it even influenced the way the King of Rock and Roll, Elvis Presley, dressed. He used to wear a jumpsuit that he referred to as "the Cisco Kid one." He wore this jumpsuit during his 1971 concerts and is featured wearing it on the cover of his 1972 Grammy-winning gospel album *He Touched Me*.[31]

The Californian funk band War reached number two on the US pop charts with their song "The Cisco Kid," which was included in their albums *The World Is a Ghetto* (1972) and *The Best of War and More*, as well as in the compilation *Sounds of the Seventies* (1983):

*The Cisco Kid was a friend of mine*
*The Cisco Kid was a friend of mine*
*He drink whiskey, Poncho drink the wine*
*He drink whiskey, Poncho drink the wine*

*We met down on the fort of Rio Grande*
*We met down on the fort of Rio Grande*
*[ … ]*

*The outlaws had us pinned down at the fort*
*The outlaws had us pinned down at the fort*
*Cisco came in blastin', drinkin' port*
*[ … ]*

*They rode the sunset, horse was made of steel*
*Chased a gringo last night through a field*
*[ … ]*

*The Cisco Kid was a friend of mine*
*[ … ]*
*The Cisco Kid he was a friend of mine*[32]

Pancho had his moment of glory with the American country singer and songwriter Don Williams, who composed "Pancho," included in the album *Turn the Page* (1998).

*Pancho, don't you like me no more*
*Pancho, to me our friendship means more*
*Pancho, please forget what I said*
*'Cause Pancho we're headin' towards our end.*
*I said someday you'll be happy with me Pancho.*
*I remember the good times when you loved me so*
*I gave you my hat and you wore your sombrero*
*And all of the times you saved me from death*

*[ … ]*
*I remember the first time when you came to town*
*Speaking in Spanish making the rounds*
*When you first saw me your face was agrin*
*And you called me the Cisco Kid.*

*Oh Pancho, you were the best.*
*I had a black horse, you had a grey*
*My horse was fastest but yours did okay*
*When it came to chasin' rustlers we'd always win*
*'Cause we were Pancho and the Cisco Kid.*
*Oh Pancho, we're headin' towards our end . . .*[33]

And even the American ska punk band, Sublime, released a song: "Cisco Kid," featured in their album *Robbin' the Hood* (1994). Their Texan vocalist, Bradley Nowell, once declared "Cisco Kid" was his favorite song on the album.

*Here's adventure*
*Here's romance*
*Here's the famous Robin Hood of the Old West*
*Cisco, the sheriff, he's getting closer*
*This way Poncho, vamonos*
*The Cisco Kid!*

*[ . . . ]*

*Now STP 1993*
*So Hollywood get out my way*
*My mom's words seems like yesterday*
*"Love Jesus, don't forget to pray"*
*She must have gone with the boss DJ*
*Right? (Don't be too sure of that fat one)*
*(Fat one?)*

*And feelin' love, skinny-ninny, coming with the 9 millimeter*
*Point your gun and bullet free*
*[ . . . ]*

*Because to me loops loops tight go (go) naturally (naturally)*
*Mom's words seem like yesterday*

*What's your name? Cisco Kid*

*Si, Poncho's name is, Poncho*

*[ . . . ]*
*If you think that Hollywood didn't get what he deserved*
*Call 808, kid, and get served*

*There's always some hombre that can't resist swappin' lead*
*Just to see if they're faster with the six gun than Cisco is*
*He he heh, those hombres find out Cisco the fastest!*
*Well that don't stop 'em from tryin', Poncho*
*[ . . . ]*
*Oh ho hoh, that one not gonna beat Cisco, either!*
*What's the matter? Can't the Cisco Kid talk for himself?*
*Is that how you got your reputation Cisco? By havin' your partner*
*build you up?*
*I make no claim to a reputation señor and no one has to talk for*
*me*
*The Cisco Kid, heh. The kid part fits you from the way you act*
*I've meet with your kind before*
*You are foolin' hombre if you think he will not fight you*
*You're making big talk for an hombre who won't fight*
*You are wrong Slade. I'll fight you any place, any time—if there*
*is a good reason*
*Well here's a fist full of reasons!*
*Is this your way you think you'll get your money?*
*Now you two quit that!*
*Just as soon as I finish off this Cisco Kid*
*[ . . . ]*
*Ha ha ha hah! Bueno, Cisco. Is that a good punch?*
*Alright you two, that's enough. Let him alone, Cisco*
*I won't forget this Cisco. I'll take this up with you another time*
*Any time hombre, I'd be glad to accommodate you*
*I'll make it soon, Cisco*
*Shut up, Cash, keep your mouth shut*
*That's what I mean, Cisco, you attract trouble like a fiddler at-*
*tracts a square dance*
*You understand why I don't want you staying in this town?*

*[...]*

We also find brief allusions to Cisco or to his image here and there. For example, American musician Mark Lindsay—lead singer for Paul Revere & The Raiders—used Cisco as the title character of the song "Arizona" (1970), within the album of the same name.

There are so many references to Cisco Kid and to Pancho that we would need a whole book for him if we would like to be exhaustive. Nevertheless, for the purpose of our goal, all these are enough to give evidence of the powerful cultural transcendence of this mythic character for all kinds of people in English-speaking culture.

### Who Inspired Whom? Zorro to Cisco Kid, or Cisco Kid to Zorro?

Obviously, both Cisco and Zorro are two very interesting characters, independent and able to survive without the other. Both have powerful roots and such a striking cultural and social impact, together and individually, that each one is worthwhile to consider without the other.

Nevertheless, one of them was first, and the other one was influenced by the first one. One of them may have inspired the creation and development of the other, as there are mutual similitudes and both of them share the same context, which is to say, the same geographic space, culture, and period of time. Both appeared almost at the same moment and covered a cultural gap that needed to be filled. Moreover, both fulfill the patterns of a Hispanic hero, with similar features we cannot but notice: they appear in films and comics dressed very smartly, in the Hispanic way; they are often found riding on horses, to whom they speak almost as best friends; they laugh and joke and mix drama with humor (even pulling their enemies' legs); they enjoy the sympathy of the common people; and they are irresistible to women. This pattern is very different from the English-heritage Western hero. The latter is serious, does not flirt, does not pull his enemy's leg, does not dress stylishly, and, of course, does not sing, as we may find Cisco or even Zorro doing, with or without a guitar. The English-heritage hero, in short, is much more sober.

Considering these shared characteristics, it is reasonable to expect that one came first, and the other one appeared when an author had seen the original one and decided to create a new character following the style of the first one, changing some details, but obviously being inspired by the existence of the first character. Which one of them was the inspiring first prototype?

Well, the dates are clear: the first character, the original—who probably inspired the author of Zorro—was Cisco Kid. Cisco Kid was created by O. Henry in 1907, while Zorro was created by Johnston McCulley in 1919. Both authors started as journalists and ended as writers, though O. Henry had a much more difficult life and had to work in many different jobs. Anyway, this means that both were readers and writers always looking for a good story and a good character.

For sure, McCulley knew Cisco Kid. He was a scriptwriter, and the short story was well known, but even if he had not read it, he had to know the two film adaptations based on Cisco Kid—*The Caballero's Way* (1914) and *The Border Terror* (1919)—the same year his character Zorro appeared for the first time in the serialized story "The Curse of Capistrano" in the pulp magazine *All-Story Weekly*.

It is easy to see the connections and how plausible it is that McCulley, seeing Cisco Kid's popularity and possibilities, decided to create another Hispanic hero, as sympathetic as Cisco Kid, but more "socially correct," developing the perfect Hispanic gentleman, converting the common antihero, Cisco Kid, to a real caballero and hero, Zorro. This does not mean that McCulley was copying O. Henry, or that one of the characters is better than the other, or purer in some sense. It only means that the original one—in the literal sense of the word "origin"—is Cisco Kid.

We also cannot ignore the very different professional approaches followed by the two authors. O. Henry has been considered the "American Guy de Maupassant" and a deep thinker. For instance, we owe the phrase "banana republic" to him, as he coined it to describe a certain type of country. He was deeply admired by Jorge Luis Borges and Edgar Alan Poe. More recently, he has also been quoted by Barack Obama as a prestigious American reference. All these facts give us the full measure of the social, literary, and cultural significance of O. Henry. McCulley, on the other hand, is considered a competent TV and film scriptwriter who also made a career in pulp magazines.

The style of both writers is present in the characters they create. O. Henry and Raoul Walsh's Cisco Kid has a dramatic and tragic dimension and has a formal treatment—both in "The Caballero's Way" and *In Old Arizona*—that allow us to compare him with other fictional characters such as Mozart's *Don Giovanni* or Shakespeare's *Othello*. Zorro has a kinder, lighter social and artistic treatment and value.

### Cisco Kid's Dimension

It is complex to establish the measure of a character that has received such different treatments by such diverse authors, and in such unequal media and formats over the course of a whole century–all the more so when we pay attention to the ambiguity that characterizes the character and all the different interpretations to which it may lead us, as we have seen in this chapter. The task is even further complicated because of the different qualites of the various stories created about Cisco Kid, as some of them are authentic precious gems and others are almost rubbish.

Nevertheless, if we try to get at the essence, what we find is a character who evolves from being a cruel and cold outlaw, a sadist bandit and desperado, an assassin of the woman he loves, to a nice fellow who steals money for the poor and is a gallant and gay cavalier—in short, becoming the American Robin Hood, someone so popular that he is part of the collective imaginary of all the generations who have lived in the United States and in Mexico in the twentieth century, and who has become a mythical figure within the Western genre, a very meaningful icon, and a legendary character.

Moreover, this character gives content and dignity to the "American Olympus," completing it with a prototype that will be enlightening and useful for many Americans who, without characters like Cisco Kid or Zorro, would have been condemned to see American Westerns where Hispanics were never heroes, played only secondary roles, and were usually identified with the "fat, lazy, dirty, ignorant, greasers with ragged mustaches" described by Nevins.

But how did it happen? How did he go from being a cold monster to a nice fellow? Recall that O. Henry used the word "caballero" in a very critical way: he comes to tell us that if being a "caballero" is being like Cisco Kid, God save us from caballeros! According to him, the caballero's way is the way of a bandit and a cold killer, a vain and simple monster able to shoot Mexicans for the pleasure of it and to kill a woman because his pride was hurt—for pure pride, disdain, and revenge, not even jealousy. The irony of the title is obvious, and he leaves it plainly clear. But the popular Cisco Kid is not like that.

Who is the real one? The original Cisco Kid or the popular one? Additionally, after so many recreations of the character and with so many authors involved in such a radical change, who is the real author?

The answers to these questions are suggested in the previous ideas expressed at the beginning of this chapter. The audience response is nowadays considered even more important than the author's intention. Most of us are conscious of how different audiences appropriate works and characters, giving a new meaning to what previously was the property of the author. Agreeing or not with Roland Barthes's and Michel Foucault's theories, we cannot ignore their influence in the way most analysts currently understand literary and cinematographic works and characters, and how the former authority of the author has given way to the power of the audiences. Cisco Kid is a good example of this.

To conclude, audiences have appropriated Cisco Kid, reinventing him, making him the hero they wanted to have, the one that their hearts and their minds wanted to enjoy, respect, and even love. The final author of Cisco Kid is the American society, telling the different media how they wanted the character to be, and that they were ready to pay for watching or reading about the Cisco Kid they felt he was like. Of course, the character is inspired by the original version, but he has evolved into what most people wanted him to be. And no matter if he was called Goodall or Chicuello, he is a Hispanic hero because this is the way he is understood and felt.

# Chapter 4

# Zorro

HOLLYWOOD WESTERNS have certainly reaped a bounteous harvest from the offshoots of the lateral and diffuse root systems created by the story of Don Diego de la Vega, a Spaniard of noble birth, raised in the Los Angeles area of California.[1] In his study of the Hispanic image on the silver screen, Alfred Charles Richard calls Zorro the "most enduring of Hispanic Heroes," although it must be noted that the Cisco Kid character preceded him on film by six years, first appearing in a 1914 movie.[2] It may be that Richard differentiates between Zorro and Cisco in terms of their heroism, as in the original O. Henry story of Cisco Kid, he was anything but a hero: "He killed for the love of it—because he was quick-tempered—to avoid arrest—for his own amusement—any reason that came to his mind would suffice."[3] In Western movies, Cisco has been "alternately, bad, good, and good-bad," and the 1914 film maintains the name of the original, "The Caballero's Way."[4] Zorro, however, is always heroic. Both Zorro and Cisco have had long, varied, and successful incarnations.

Zorro and Cisco both began in print. The Zorro character manifested itself for the first time in the text of Johnston McCulley's *The Curse of Capistrano* (1919), then in film (1920), and subsequently on television, which in turn resulted in action figures, costumes, and other toys. Costume shops regularly advertise not only the black pants, shirt, mask, and cape but also the sword, hat, and even the mustache.

Comic strips and video games are other venues where Zorro appears. Who knows what future incarnations the long-lasting and continuing fascination with Zorro will produce? The attraction of the creation was almost instantaneous. Just one year after first appearing in print, the Zorro character inspired a celluloid embodiment. It was 1920 when Hollywood began its captivation with Zorro, in an early silent film starring Douglas Fairbanks Sr. This first movie, titled *The Mark of Zorro*, was such a big hit that it broke the box office record of the time for a single day. Douglas Fairbanks Sr. produced and starred in it; he even participated in the writing, although he used two of his middle names, Elton Thomas, as his nom de plume in the credits (Douglas Elton Thomas Fairbanks was his full name). This first celluloid Zorro was to influence not only future Zorro movies and television series but also other Western heroes, thus establishing its significance as an important root in the multifaceted development of the Western.

*The Mark of Zorro* (1920) is set in the early part of the nineteenth century in old Spanish California, where Don Alejandro, Don Diego's father, is dealing with the corrupt administration of Governor Alvarado and his villainous henchman, Captain Juan Ramon. Although he acts the fop, Don Diego has secretly donned a mask and takes steps to protect the people from their oppressors. One problem for future films is that at the end of this film Don Diego reveals himself. *The Mark of Zorro* was so successful that it was remade twice, each new generation producing its own version: Tyrone Power played Zorro once (1940), and some three decades later Frank Langella assumed the mask and wielded the whip (1974). The century was almost over before an actual Spaniard played this Spanish hero. In 1998, Antonio Banderas reprised the role. This time the title was a little changed, turning the *r* in *Mark* into an *s* for *Mask*. *The Mask of Zorro* was the first time Banderas played Zorro; the second time was in a film titled *The Legend of Zorro*, which was released in 2005, some seven years later.

The original silent film provided a strong root system for the development of future Zorros and other Western heroes. In particular, Fairbanks's noteworthy brand of athleticism set a paradigm for the future Zorros. The film shows him dueling, running, jumping, and riding. It also established the archetypal Zorro gesture of carving a *Z* in the flesh of his enemies or elsewhere to announce his presence. Each dialogue screen of this silent film was decorated with a sword in the upper left-hand corner and a $Z$ in the lower right. Zorro marking his opponents is a very fitting Western gesture, as, in a way, it echoes the branding of cattle. Cattle are branded to ensure that they are recognized as belonging to one herd or to another. Zorro brands his enemies to ensure that they recognize his dominance and cannot deny his presence.

Another archetypal Zorro gesture, born in this film, is leaving his sword stuck in things, such as a tree in one instance and a wall or a ceiling in another. Again, this is to serve notice to his enemies that he is present, or, as he says when he throws his sword into a wall, "till I need you again."[5] Like a number of other heroes in adventure novels and comic books, in some of the stories Don Diego keeps his identity as Zorro secret, acting the effete, dandy gentleman for the public. In this he is not unlike Sir Percival Blakeney, the hero of Baroness Orczy's Scarlet Pimpernel action series, or Clark Kent, Superman's mild-mannered reporter whose mask is to act quite unlike his heroic reality (although why Lois Lane does not recognize his face is a mystery to us). Of course, these are generalizations; the Zorro phenomenon has produced so many offshoots—not only in film but also in radio, television, and even video and computer games—that it would be impossible to maintain a consistency of characteristics.

The Spanish heritage of Zorro's family is marked in a number of ways. In the initial scenes of the Fairbanks film, Don Diego has just returned from Spain. In a tavern a man recounts to his compadres a story about how he was beating someone when a masked man appeared and carved a $Z$ into his face. He displays the scar to the crowd. Also in the tavern is one Sergeant Gonzales, who struts and bellows about. While Sergeant Gonzales is bullying everyone in the tavern, kicking over chairs and their occupants, Don Diego arrives, preceded into the room by his umbrella to emphasize his being a bit of a dandy. He orders a pot of honey for himself and drinks for everyone. In this scene Sergeant Gonzales blusters about, showing off to the patrons, saying what he will do to Zorro, as the audience is treated to the comedy of the dramatic irony that Gonzales does not realize that in talking to Don Diego, he is talking to Zorro. Another reminder to the audience that this is New Spain and all this should be spoken in Spanish is when a man comes to post a sign announcing a reward for the capture of Zorro, *vivo o muerto* (alive or dead). Initially, the sign is in Spanish, but its English translation appears immediately on screen for the audience.[6]

Zorro is a hero for the underdog, be he a Spanish peon, a Native American, or, in some cases, even a priest. After his "dandy" introduction, Don Diego's initial appearance in the Zorro costume occurs early in *The Mark of Zorro*, when Gonzales begins beating a native worker in the tavern. Zorro appears, smoking, and uncharacteristically threatens the crowd with a gun. When they retreat, he puts up the gun and challenges Gonzales with a rapier. Another of Zorro's characteristic manners is introduced here, as Zorro makes fun of Gonzales during their fight. He sits and throws beans at Gonzales, clearly toying with him, as the men laugh. Zorro's remarkable athleticism is demonstrated as he jumps on the mantle and over tables. When asked about his remarkable swordsmanship, Zorro explains that he learned it in Spain.

This version of the Zorro story has Zorro entering his home through a hidden entry. There he encounters Bernardo, who is humorously identified as the ideal servant, one who can hear but can't speak. Here again is a model for such future heroes as Batman, whose Bat Cave is known only to his trusted butler. It may be no coincidence that in the Batman story Bruce Wayne's parents had just seen this movie, *The Mark of Zorro*, when they were murdered. A feature of this hidden area is that Don Diego has a peephole that allows him to see his father. It is also a space where he can ditch his Zorro trappings and put on his more effete clothing, which he does a number of times in the story.

The plot, such as it is, incorporates a love story along with its main thrust of a fight for justice. Don Diego is chastised by his father for his idleness and his failure to win a wife. The older De La Vega informs his son that he has written to the Pulido family and told them that his son will come courting. The courting scene is played for laughs as Don Diego presents a very bloodless courtier, doing magic tricks to divert. He invites all the family to his home.

Following up with a strong love ingredient, the 1940 version of *The Mark of Zorro*, which starred Tyrone Power in the title role, includes Linda Darnell as Lolita Quintero, the niece of Don Luis Quintero, the man who has replaced Don Diego's father as Alcalde of Los Angeles, thus giving the story a hint of a Romeo and Juliet allusion of opposing families.

Another typical move of the Western hero is that he does not mount his horse using the stirrup: he leaps onto it either from the ground or some high location, such as a balcony. Here again, Zorro provides the model. After having courted Lolita Pulido in her family garden, he makes his getaway jumping on his horse over the garden wall. This is in keeping with his general athleticism and remarkable energy. Zorro never just walks into a room or enters unobtrusively. He swings onto second stories, often using his whip as a makeshift rope. He bounds into the church and then exits leaping over walls. If a horse is not a handy mount, he jumps onto a donkey.

The Spanish pedigree is emphasized when Zorro castigates the soldiers for their lack of action. He reminds them of their inheritance of the blood of Aragon, the legacy of Castille. He inspires them, reminding them that they are "caballeros." They respond by raising their swords and pledging to fight for justice—"Justice for all." Setting the tone for future Zorros and other Western heroes, Zorro rides to the rescue in a number of instances. He rescues the Pulidos from jail and then Lolita from Captain Ramon. Finally, Don Diego reveals himself as Zorro and carves a *Z* in Ramon's forehead. When Zorro throws his sword into the wall with the words, "Till I need you again," the stage is set for future adventures. This, too, prefigures other Western series, where the audience knows that when a wrong needs to be addressed, a hero such as the Lone Ranger, Hopalong Cassidy, Roy Rogers, or Lash LaRue will arrive on the scene.

The success of the first Zorro film assured that there would be a sequel. In this case, Douglas Fairbanks plays not only the original Zorro, Don Diego, but also his son, Don Cesar. Still in the silent film era, *Don Q, Son of Zorro* was based not on a McCulley story, but on a novel called *Don Q's Love Story.* It was produced in 1925.

The Spanish heritage of the Vega family is again reinforced in *Don Q, Son of Zorro.* The opening text of the film emphasizes the Spanish pedigree of the De Vega lineage. It states that a De Vega was with Balboa when he first set eyes on the Pacific Ocean, a De Vega was with Pizarro when he conquered Peru, and a young De Vega died fighting in the conquest of Mexico with Cortez. In fact, it might be hard to call this a Western as it is set almost entirely—except for a brief scene back in California—in Spain. Notwithstanding this setting, it is made clear that California is the De Vega home but that the sons and heirs return to Spain to round out their educations. In this case it is Don Cesar, who is the son of the original Zorro, spending some time in what one assumes is Madrid, as the queen and her court are there. And while one might take the westerner out of the West, he emphasizes that his prowess with the whip and rapier were taught to him by his father, whom he identifies as "the Greatest Man in America." When Don Cesar is presented to the queen, he is called a "westerner." There is a De Vega ancestral home outside the city, but it is in ruins. It is, however, an important setting, as the climactic scenes occur there.

The plot begins with Don Cesar showing off his abilities with a whip. In the various high jinks that follow—including a bull set loose on the crowd and Don Cesar corralling it—he is brought to the attention of Archduke Paul, cousin to the queen. In search of fun, Archduke Paul decides to have a night on the town with Cesar. One Sebastian, a captain of the Queen's Guard, is sent to accompany them, and they jokingly refer to him as their duenna.[7]

Douglas Fairbanks Jr. followed his father's film path as a swashbuckling hero, though he never played Zorro. At one time, there was a plan for father and son to star together in a film, tentatively titled either *Zorro Rides Again* or *Zorro and Son*. However, that never came to be. An interesting side note is that Douglas Fairbanks Jr. was as heroic in real life as the characters he portrayed on film. His dangerous exploits during World War II earned him a number of medals, including the US Navy Legion of Merit with a Bronze V for Valor, a Silver Star for Valor, and French, Italian, and British medals as well.

In the 1930s, the Zorro root system flowered in some unusual ways. *Zorro Rides Again*, released by Hal Roach Studios in 1937, is an interesting melding of the old and the new. It is a twelve-chapter Republic serial. The success of this multi-sectioned Zorro offering is evidenced by the fact that Republic produced four more serials in short succession: *Zorro's Fighting Legions* followed several years later in 1939. Perhaps World War II delayed the next series as it came in 1944 as *Zorro's Black Whip*. However, there were two more serials produced in the 1940s: *Son of Zorro* (1947) and *Ghost of Zorro* (1949). The setting for *Zorro Rides Again* is again Mexico and California, but not the Mexico and California of the original Don Diego's days; in this time period, there are airplanes and multistory buildings. This establishes the premise that there are multiple Zorros. In some cases, it is a matter of heredity, as in *Ghost of Zorro* (1949), when the Zorro identity is assumed by the original American's great-grandson. In other situations, as in *The Mask of Zorro*, it is a protégé taught by the original Zorro.

There are a number of interesting surprises in these Republic serials. In the first, *Zorro Rides Again*, Duncan Reynaldo, who later played the Cisco Kid, plays Reynaldo, a loyal friend of Zorro's. He is the one who had mentored James Vega, the original Zorro's great-grandson, when he was a boy. He proudly proclaims, "I teach him many things."[8] This includes knowledge of the hidden passageway behind the painting of the original Zorro. Reynaldo often accompanies Zorro on his adventures. These Republic serials use an interesting mix of the modern and the Old West. Each chapter begins with a horseman riding across a desert-like countryside.

In some cases, the mercurial identity of Zorro is announced with the opening credits, as in *Zorro Rides Again*. This is "a New Zorro," it proclaims. This Zorro is to be "more dashing, more courageous, and more Romantic" than his famous ancestor. At least a hereditary connection is maintained. John Carroll plays this version of Zorro. The ongoing premise of this twelve-chapter serial is that James Vega returns to the home of his uncle, Manuel Vega, who wants him to be a Zorro. And in a way he follows the path of the original by assuming a weak and passive mask at first. It is not till his uncle is shot that Zorro doffs his mask and reveals himself to the dying Manuel, who then sighs happily. The problem to be dealt with is that the family interest in the California-Yucatan Railroad is being threatened by a big banker named Marsden, who wants to gain control.[9] Marsden employs a man named El Lobo, who heads a group of ne'er-do-wells who do Marsden's illegal biddings. They blow up California-Yucatan Railroad properties and damage the trains. Typical of this quasi-modern yet traditional Western, El Lobo's group rides horses, while the current Vega family rides in an automobile.[10]

In keeping with the archetypal pattern of the serial, the individual chapters often end with a cliff-hanger. That is, at the end of each chapter the audience is left with a scene in which it appears that the hero will be killed or severely maimed. One example is when Zorro is trying to prevent El Lobo's gang from setting off a time bomb to blow up the supplies of the California-Yucatan Railroad. In the final scene of this chapter, the warehouse blows up. It is not until the next chapter that we find out that Zorro had managed to climb down into the cellar seconds before the explosion. Again *à la* the serial tradition, in the beginning of each new chapter the audience is shown the final scenes of the previous chapter. Prior to Zorro being in the warehouse alone with one of Lobo's gang, Zorro's love interest, Joyce, almost finds the bomb a number of times. Each time she is about to open the stove door that hides it, someone calls her or diverts her attention. In another of the cliff-hangers, in a chapter appropriately named "Unmasked," the final scene shows Lobo reaching to pull off the mask of the helpless Zorro. Of course, Reynaldo shows up just in time. The case of the mask is also an inconsistency across the various Zorro films. In some, the black mask covers the entire face; in others, it merely covers the eyes. Some finales include an unmasking, while in other films the identity of Zorro remains a mystery.

Reinforcing the traditional Western character of this serial, even though it is set in the contemporary era of its issue, the scenery is often a landscape of high mesas, rocky hills, culverts, and canyons. Horse and rider often slide down the side of hills where there is little vegetation. Certain Western locations are mentioned, such as El Paso, but are not shown.

In this serial, the secret entry for Zorro and Reynaldo is through a picture of the original Zorro. This allows him to accomplish a number of helpful acts. In one chapter, Zorro receives a written offer from Marsden. Naturally, the document is signed. Zorro, using modern technology, erases everything but the signature and then takes the signed paper up to his room, where he retypes it as authorization to pay for supplies for the railroad. Another instance of how this serial incorporates both the traditional and the modern is the use of the shortwave radio. Zorro is able to forestall much of El Lobo's chicanery because he and Reynaldo tap into the radio communication between Lobo and Marsden. For all of the inclusion of modern technology, however, the importance of Zorro's horse, here named El Rey (The King), is underlined. This horse is black and white, unlike earlier Zorro horses. He also plays important roles in helping. In the chapter titled "Tapped Phone Lines," El Rey whinnies a warning in one scene. In another he frightens a bad guy. In the final scene, it is El Rey who stomps on El Lobo, then plays the important role of nudging Zorro/James into the arms of Joyce for the serial closing.[11]

The fertility of the Zorro root system is so potent that it is not even necessary to *have* Zorro in the film *Zorro's Black Whip*. In this movie, starring Linda Stirling, the word "Zorro" is never uttered, although the main character is strangely similar to Zorro. Its protagonist is a woman. She is called "The Black Whip," and her actions are often replicative of Zorro.[12]

By 1940, Hollywood thought audiences were ready for a new Zorro movie, also titled *The Mark of Zorro*. In this case, Tyrone Power, an actor of strong box-office appeal, appears as the masked hero. Twentieth Century Fox was the producer of this film. The strong Spanish roots of our hero are underlined as this version begins not in California but in Madrid. There we see Don Diego with other "young blades," as the movie terms them, learning the basics of fencing and horsemanship. Don Diego's fellow students call him the "California cockerel" and constantly challenge him to duels. Interestingly, although the lead roles were not played by actors of Hispanic heritage, Rouben Mamoulian, the director, insisted that all the extras be either Spaniards or Mexicans. Linda Darnell, another Hollywood favorite of the time, plays the romantic lead.[13]

The advent of television gave rise to numerous Zorro incarnations. While technically one could say this book is about the "Hollywood" Western, it was often in Hollywood that the films shown on television were produced. In the case of television's Zorro, it was a significant Hollywood studio that produced the most successful Zorro series, one that was initially broadcast on the Disney Channel five days a week.

Reinforcing the strong Hispanic roots of the Zorro figure, a made-for-television movie, *The Mark of Zorro* (1974), actually begins with Don Diego in Spain exercising with other cadets at the military academy. Drinking with them, he announces his imminent return to California, as he has had ominous news from home. Prior to leaving, however, he heaves his rapier into one of the ceiling beams, a signature Zorro move. While Frank Langella plays Zorro, the film boasts two major Hispanic actors in key roles: Ricardo Montalban plays Captain Esteban and Gilbert Roland plays Don Alejandro Vega.[14]

Another major contribution that the character of Zorro and Zorro films made to the Western is the introduction of the whip as a weapon of choice for the hero. Of course, the standard Hollywood Western hero is quick with a gun. The quick draw is another of those wonderful Hollywood fantasies. Never mind that the reality of those times was that six-shooters were unreliable unless one aimed carefully and probably balanced one hand with the other. (One tale from old El Paso is of Marshal Dallas Stoudenmire, who was ambushed walking out of a saloon. The would-be assassin emptied his gun at the marshal, missing completely. Chasing him, Stoudenmire also shot numerous times. The sad irony is that the only people killed were some innocent bystanders.) Zorro's use of the whip and the rapier gives him a unique quality. The whip was then appropriated by such Western heroes as Lash LaRue and Indiana Jones. One of the funnier scenes in more recent films is when Indiana confronts a rather large saber-waving villain and exchanges his whip for the quicker and deadlier gun.

Since the setting of the original Zorro film is an era where gentlemen fenced, the rapier is also a preferred weapon for Zorro. It is with the rapier that Zorro carves his initial into the bodies of his enemies or on walls. Sometimes, as in the pre-credit scenes or the closing scenes of the movie, Zorro simply slashes a fiery *Z* into the atmosphere. As mentioned earlier, gunfights are mostly a Hollywood invention. In real life, Wild Bill Hickock, who was one of the few gunfighters who was a good shot, was murdered by being shot in the back of the head while he was playing cards in a saloon. The cards he held were aces and eights, thereafter called a "dead man's hand." In other words, villains in reality knew better than to challenge the hero directly. John Wesley Hardin is another gunfighter who was killed by being shot in the back in an El Paso saloon. Using the rapier, as Zorro does, thus involves a more even-handed (pun intended) approach to heroism. Zorro faces his enemies directly; the battle is face-to-face. Yes, guns are used in Zorro films, but mostly by the bad guys. And while Zorro is shot many times, he is never hit, true to Hollywood reality.

In addition, the Zorro character has inspired not only American films but also movies in Mexico and Europe. Spain's 1953 *La montaña sin ley* is one of the first instances of a Spanish actor playing Zorro. In 1962, Spain followed up with *La Venganza del Zorro*. One of the more recent additions to the Zorro phenomenon is a 2005 novel by Chilean author Isabel Allende; her work can be called a prequel as it tells the story of Zorro before McCulley's *The Curse of Capistrano,* which inspired the first Zorro film. In Brian Garfield's extensive catalogue of Western films, he includes three Zorro films in an appendix titled "The Made-For-TV and Spaghetti Westerns."[15] He describes them as equivalent to earlier B movies. The three Zorro films listed here are captioned as SI, meaning that they are Spanish or Italian, that is, Spaghetti Westerns. One *Zorro* came out in 1961, and Garfield points out that it is "badly dubbed."[16] Following in 1963 was *Zorro the Avenger* (Frank Latimore stars in both). This one Garfield labels "Spaghettidiocy."[17] Garfield's evaluation of the 1975 *Zorro* takes the movie makers to task for not even crediting the McCulley original. Surprisingly, as he unearthed these little-known Zorro films, Garfield lists only *The Mark of Zorro* (1940), starring Tyrone Power, in the main section of the book, although some omissions can be explained by his time restriction of 1928–1981. His evaluation of that film is that the duel between Tyrone Power and Basil Rathbone is "marvelous."[18]

As pointed out earlier, it is ironic that so many years and versions of Zorro passed before an actual Spanish actor played the role. *The Mask of Zorro* (1998), the first Zorro film with a Spanish actor in the starring role, begins with Zorro slashing a fiery *Z* across the screen before the title. An important aspect of this film is that it emphasizes the fact that Zorro does not have to be Don Diego or any of his family. In this film, while Anthony Hopkins does play the original in the beginning of the movie, he is succeeded by a boy he meets as he is standing up for the people. In the opening scene, California has been lost to Spain because of the Mexican Revolution and the last Spanish governor, Don Rafael Montero, is hesitant to relinquish power. Here again, as is his wont, Zorro uses his whip to prevent injustice. The governor has set up a firing squad for three men who are not necessarily guilty of anything. As Zorro's whip pulls the rifles toward the captain of the firing squad, who is shot instead of the bound men, fighting breaks out, and the two boys help by knocking a statue over on the governor's guards. Zorro thanks the boys and gives them an amulet. The crowd roars for Zorro, and he cuts a *Z* in the governor's throat. He jumps on his horse, and the movie shows the quintessential Spanish equestrian shot, as he is silhouetted against the sun as the horse rears.[19]

In considering the key role played by Zorro, one has to appreciate that, unlike many of the other Western heroes who had only one manifestation or inspired only one radio or television series, Zorro had multiple incarnations on radio, on television, and in film. For example, Gene Autry was a key Western hero whose career included not only movies but also radio and television; however, that lasted only as long as he played the role. He made a fortune, but the role of this singing cowboy began and ended with him. The same is true for another famous cowboy, Roy Rogers. Known as "King of the Cowboys," he, too, starred in movies, radio, and television. Not only that, but his horse Trigger and his wife Dale Evans also became famous. Clothing, comic books, and games all bore his name. Nonetheless, his character lasted only as long as he could play the role. The point here is that the role of Zorro is not dependent on any one actor. Like a strong root system, he gives rise to multiple flowerings. The idea of multiple Zorros is clearly articulated in *The Mask of Zorro*, since one Zorro teaches another how to become one and that one is not related to him. This Don Diego has a daughter, not a son. She, of course, demonstrates her roots, as she is quite handy with a rapier.

An irony in this film, wherein a Spanish actor plays Zorro for the first time, is that it is not Antonio Banderas who plays the original Zorro—that is, Anthony Hopkins. In *The Mask of Zorro*, twenty years pass from the time of the opening scene, where the two brothers are given an amulet by Zorro. The boys are not Spaniards, but of the Mexican peasant class in California.

Chapter 5

# The Spanish Western

UNEXPECTEDLY, when the Golden Age of Hollywood was almost over and the Western as a genre seemed to be on a slow decline, many Westerns were filmed in the 1960s and 1970s in Spain.

This enormous production of Westerns in Spain was absolutely surprising for many reasons. First of all, because who could imagine that the Europeans would feel such an interest in a genre that seemed to be the authentic and genuinely American genre, dealing with American history, its epic, its roots, and its search for its identity? Second, because whoever would dare to do such a thing had to be crazy to compete with storytellers of the magnitude of John Ford, Howard Hawks, Fritz Lang, King Vidor, Anthony Mann, Raoul Walsh, Henry King, William Wyler, Stanley Donen, Nicholas Ray, John Sturges, John Huston, Sam Peckinpah, etc. Third, because after World War II everything changed; the interests, principles, and values were different. In less than a decade, people changed from pursuing the "American dream" to becoming hippies, and people shifted from adoring musicians like Frank Sinatra and Ella Fitzgerald to being fans of "their Satanic Majesties," the Rolling Stones and Janis Joplin, for example. In this new landscape, shooting Westerns did not seem to be the best idea, as who among these new citizens would enjoy new stories of gunfighters, sheriffs, bandits, and lonely heroes trying to make justice not only in the far West but also in the far past?

Moreover, at that time, political relationships between Spain and the United States were very bad. Spain, being then ruled by the dictator Francisco Franco, was not well considered in the United States. Americans were so sensitive with regard to this fact that, when giving money to most European countries after World War II with the Marshall Plan (the European Recovery Program), not a dollar was given to Spain, generating a big disappointment among the Spanish population, a situation masterfully portrayed in the film *Bienvenido, Mister Marshall* (1953), directed by the superb Spanish filmmaker Luis García Berlanga.

In those years, Spain was internationally disregarded by most countries because of its political regime, becoming a poor and isolated country. Who could imagine that the Western was going to flourish again, and in Spain of all places?

But, considered more carefully, we can see that it was almost a natural evolution. Why? Because first of all, Westerns were telling stories that mostly happened in the West of the United States, in a land that was formerly a Spanish territory. This is evident not only in history but also by the names still in use in these places (Los Angeles, California, San Diego, El Paso, Rio Grande, Nevada, Las Vegas, Arizona, Sacramento, Santa Fe, Colorado, etc.); by the culture (music, architecture, food, clothes, etc.); and even by the people (many residents are descendants of Spanish people mixed with Indigenous inhabitants). So, inevitably, the frame, the land, the scenery, the backdrop, and even the language of an important number of the people living there are connected with Spain, demonstrating that the roots of Westerns are deeply connected with the Spanish culture and the Spanish people.

Second, because, astonishingly, the southwestern states of the United States have a landscape, remarkably similar to the countryside we find in different provinces of Spain, especially in Almería.

Third, because Spain is a land historically crossed by most civilizations and races along the centuries due to its geographical emplacement. Spanish people are thus the result of a big mix of races, with inhabitants of different sizes, colors, and types. In fact, Spain is a genuine melting pot, just like the United States, providing in this way the variety of types of human beings that traditionally appear in a Western. In sum, it is in fact very easy to film Westerns in Spain, as it provided not only the old roots and the landscape, but also the human resources with an acceptable similarity to the people who lived originally in the Far West.

Moreover, Spain during Francoism, in the 1950s and 1960s, was very poor compared with other European countries and with the United States, something that was a clear incentive for shooting in Spain because films that would have cost a lot of money in other places were affordable in Spain. For example, the Spanish Army provided thousands of troops to serve as extras for only two dollars per day, horses included. Ted Richmond, producer of *Salomon and Sheba* (1959), directed by King Vidor, said, "Our collaboration with the Spanish Army, including more than 3,000 movie extras, has cost $80,000, and a similar display in America would have cost $1,600,000."[1] The Spanish newspaper *El Socialista,* issued in France (Toulouse) by Spaniards living in exile in the 1950s, published an article on October 29, 1959, titled, "Hollywood y Franquilandia. Ocasión: se alquila ejército" ("Hollywood and Francoland. Opportunity: Army to Rent!").

And besides, in Almería the sun does not disappear until 8:00 p.m., or even until 10:00 p.m. in summer, something that made Almería a natural movie set, just like California in the beginning of the twentieth century. In both cases this was a very interesting factor to be considered by moviemakers. This was another amazing parallelism, as it also happened with landscapes, people, culture, language, etc.

Though these Spanish Westerns were international co-productions, all of them were shot in Spain and many times edited and mixed there, too. They were co-produced with the United States or with other European countries, mainly with Italy, but also with France, Belgium, Germany, Austria, and even Yugoslavia, and they were very different from the American Westerns. So, we may justly by speaking of a new type of Westerns: the European Western.

It presented an unusual way of telling the history of the Far West, and even a new audio visual language was developed. This new style is so different from the classical one that we can affirm that most of us, just watching ten minutes of a Western, can say whether it is a "modern" European one or a "classical" American one. These films were so different and fruitful that they were recognized as a new subgenre, which received the familiar name "Spaghetti Western."

### The Unexpected "European Hollywood": Spain

The Motion Picture Export Association of America (MPEA) had a problem in Spain after the Spanish Civil War: Franco's government instituted severe restrictions on the distribution of American motion pictures, and they had to find a way both for liberalizing the market and for recovering all the frozen funds that were not possible to take out of Spain after the Civil War.

In fact, as a consequence of this, a long embroilment between the MPEA and the Franco regime arose in the postwar era, a conflict that is deeply analyzed by Pablo León Aguinaga in his book *Sospechosos habituales: El cine norteamericano, Estados Unidos y la España franquista, 1939-1960*, and by Neal Moses Rosendorf in *Hollywood in Madrid: American Film Producers and the Franco Regime in the 1950s-60s*.[2] Little by little a solution was found, thanks to two meaningful men who helped to speed up the process and find a solution: George Ornstein and Samuel Bronston.

Ornstein was the United Artists (UA) representative in Spain (and the son-in-law of UA majority shareholder Mary Pickford). He managed to arrange for UA funds to get unblocked in Spain, but in exchange, UA guaranteed that this recovered money would be invested in producing or co-producing films in Spain.

As a result, between 1955 and 1958, UA was able to strike favorable deals to make possible several mega-productions filmed wholly in Spain. *The Film Daily* reported in 1960 that UA had risen since the early 1950s to be the number-one American film producer and distributor operating in Spain. And thanks to this agreement, films such as *Around the World in 80 Days* (1956), directed by Michael Todd, and *The Pride and the Passion* (1957) by Stanley Kramer were shot in Spain, starting a collaboration that would increase over the years, converting Spain into the set *par excellence* of the Spaghetti Western.

Ornstein's success was such that in the 1960s he was awarded both the "Mérito Civil" medal and Spain's highest civilian honor, the "Order of Isabel la Católica." Moreover, Ornstein paved the way for Samuel Bronston.

Bronston had worked for Metro-Goldwin-Mayer and Columbia

Pictures and later founded his own production company, Samuel Bronston Productions, becoming a pioneer in locating epic-scale productions in Spain.[3] The producer moved his family from New York to Madrid, and like Ornstein, he used frozen funds and cheap costs for shooting in Spain to produce epic films such as *King of Kings* (1961) by Nicholas Ray, *El Cid* (1961) by Anthony Mann, *55 Days at Peking* (1963) by Nicholas Ray, *Circus World* (1964) by Henry Hathaway, and *The Fall of the Roman Empire* (1964) by Anthony Mann.

Bronston also received the Order of Isabel la Católica. He was exceptionally skilled at networking and making business connections. But the combination of the cost of the construction of the film studios and the box-office failure of his last film, *The Fall of the Roman Empire*, left him in financial difficulties, and in 1964 he had to stop all business activities. He owed money to Pierre S. Dupont and to Paramount, among others. After bankruptcy in 1964 and criminal prosecution because of the scandal that surged when being accused of corruption, his film career was ruined. The Franco regime helped Bronston after his fall, giving him a moratorium on his debts, though finally he had to leave the country in 1973 with his bills still unpaid.

To Franco's minister of information and tourism, Manuel Fraga Iribarne, the American films made in Spain were "Spanish films" distributed by Hollywood, and they were not only an element for activating the economy but also, and perhaps even more importantly, a tool for creating a positive international image of Spain.

Great movies such as *Mr. Arkadin* (1955) by Orson Welles, *Richard III* (1957) by Laurence Olivier, *Fiesta* (1957) by Henry King, *Moby Dick* (1958) by John Huston, *Suddenly, Last Summer* (1959) by Joseph L. Mankiewicz, *Salomon and Sheba* (1959) by King Vidor, *Spartacus* (1960) by Stanley Kubrick, *Lawrence of Arabia* (1962) and *Doctor Zhivago* (1965) by David Lean, part of *Cleopatra* (1963) by Joseph L. Mankiewicz, *Chimes at Midnight* (1965) by Orson Welles, *The Hill* (1965) by Sidney Lumet, *Battle of the Bulge* (1966) by Ken Annakin, *Camelot* (1967) by Joshua Logan, *Shalako* (1968) by Edward Dmytryck, *The Battle of Britain* (1969) by Guy Hamilton, *Krakatoa, East of Java* (1969) by Bernard L. Kowalski,

*Patton* (1970) by Franklin Schaffner, *How I Won the War* (1967) and *Robin and Marian* (1976) by Richard Lester, *The Wind and the Lion* (1975) by John Milius, among others, were filmed in Spain. This list represents a gorgeous filmography, to which we have to add all the Spaghetti Westerns made in Spain, among them, of course, the "Dollars Trilogy": *A Fistful of Dollars* (1964), *For a Few Dollars More* (1965), and *The Good, the Bad and the Ugly* (1966), by Sergio Leone, and also most parts of Leone's *Once Upon a Time in the West* (1968) and *Duck, You Sucker!* (1971).

César Antonio Molina, writer, university professor, and Minister of Culture in Spain, declared:

"Fue mucho lo que hizo Hollywood en España, probablemente sin saberlo: meternos dentro de la historia del cine universal, meternos dentro de la política internacional, poco a poco, ayudarnos a que se rompiera la autarquía, y a que España iniciara un camino nuevo y diferente, ayudar a los profesionales del cine español, y abrirnos, en definitiva, a abrirnos al mundo."

(Probably without even knowing it, Hollywood did a lot in Spain: they introduced us to the universal history of cinema, they put us again within international politics, little by little, contributing to the breakdown of the autarchy, and helping Spain to initiate a new and different path, helping the Spanish film professional, and helping us, ultimately, to open to the world.)[4]

In the 1950s–1960s, and part of the 1970s, Madrid became a "small Hollywood" where film stars as Cary Grant, Frank Sinatra, Sophia Loren, Charlton Heston, Ava Gardner, David Niven, George Cukor, Kirk Douglas, Jean Simmons, Orson Welles, Elizabeth Taylor, Richard Burton, Sidney Lumet, Laurence Olivier, Charles Laughton, Sean Connery, Brigitte Bardot, Peter Ustinov, Audrey Hepburn, Tyrone Power, Omar Sharif, David Lean, Peter O'Toole, Tony Curtis, Julie Christie, Glen Ford, Claudia Cardinale, Samuel Fuller, Geraldine Chaplin, Raquel Welch, Clint Eastwood, Ursula Andress, Gina Lollobrigida, Gregory Peck, Anthony Quinn, John Wayne, and Rita Hayworth were part of its landscape. Chicote and

Castellana Hilton, and the dining room of the Jockey Club, were places where one could meet movie stars, famous directors, writers, and musicians, giving Madrid an unprecedented air of cosmopolitanism.

The movies were filmed in several Spanish locations: Madrid, Denia, Castellón, Peñíscola, Pamplona, Las Matas, Hoyo de Manzanares, La Cabrera, Toledo, Luarca (Asturias), Esplugues (Barcelona), Burgos, Laredo and Santoña (both in Santander), Sevilla, Segovia, Ciudad Encantada (Cuenca), Soria, Fraga (Huesca), Talamanca de Jarama, Huelva, Guadix and La Calahorra (both in Granada), and Almería.

In spite of Samuel Bronston's ending, his works and his goals were and are recognized as significant. Like Ornstein, he prepared the way for the appearance of the Spanish Western and the Spaghetti Western, creating the foundations of an internationally meaningful film industry in Spain.

What happened in Spain, and specifically in Almería, was a distinct phenomenon for everyone, the inhabitants and the visitors. In this regard, the Egyptian actor Omar Sharif declared after playing the protagonist, together with Peter O'Toole, in *Lawrence of Arabia* (1962) by David Lean: "I 'was born' in Almería. Without Almería there would not be Omar Sharif."[5] On February 15, 1968, *The Hollywood Reporter* published an article titled, "Almeria-Movie Capital of the World," saying that the Spanish city of Almería was proclaiming itself, not entirely without justification, the "Movie Capital of the World."[6]

### The Spanish Western

As we are seeing, a prosperous film industry linked to the United States was created in Spain, an industry that, paradoxically, was related to the Franco regime and that practically disappeared when he died in 1975. It started with those independent American filmmakers who trekked to Spain to enlist the Franco regime's cooperation in producing big-budget motion pictures, but finally it became a Spanish Western film industry, as most movies filmed after Samuel Bronston's bankruptcy were Westerns.

It is difficult to classify these Westerns, as most of them were international co-productions, Spain being only one of the co-producers. In most of them we do find not only the Spanish land but also Spanish actors, both as protagonists and in secondary roles, and, of course, all the movie extras and movie specialists. We also find Spanish film directors, script writers, art directors, cameramen, sound engineers, soundmen, musicians, producers, all types of sound and lightning technicians, editors, movie hairdressers and makeup artists, clothing specialists, etc. The film sets, the furniture, the clothes: everything was made in Spain. So, the Spanish artists and technicians present in these films make them, to a large extent, "Spanish Westerns."

The large number of Spaniards involved in making these films can be identified when reading the film credits of the movies, but even this big figure would be imprecise and smaller than the real one, as it happened that most Spaniards realized that if they changed their Spanish names into English ones, they would find more work and they would be more respected, so they did so. Consequently, the number of existing Spanish artists and technicians could not be calculated only by counting the Spanish names in credits but by adding this figure to the number of English artistic names that masked many Spaniards.

This exchange of names does not have to surprise us, as most Europeans who worked in Hollywood also changed their names into English ones for the same reasons. Even the American film director John Ford did it, as his real name was the Irish name Sean Aloysius O' Feeney. In fact, most of the English names present in the film credits of the Spaghetti Westerns are pseudonyms, as Italian film crews did the same, changing their Italian names into English ones.

Anselmo Núñez Marqués, in his book *Western a la europea: Un plato que se sirve frío*, offers an interesting appendix with a long list of English pseudonyms used by these film professionals. For instance, we find that the real name of the famous, blue-eyed actor Terence Hill, who played Trinity in the film *They Call Me Trinity* (1970), is Mario Girotti.[7] His corpulent mate Bud Spencer's real name is Carlo Pedersoli, as both of them are Italians. In the same way, we find that the Spanish film director Jesús Franco changed his name into Jess Frank, Antonio del Amo into Richard Jackson, Ricardo Blasco into Richard Blask, Juan Bosh into John Wood, Miguel de la Riva into Michael Rivers, etc.

Núñez Marqués proposes two classifications for these Westerns. The first one divides them into "Gazpacho Western," "Butifarra Western," "Chorizo Western," etc., going on with the gastronomic simile of the "Spaghetti Western." The second one follows a diachronic approach and allocates these Westerns into three periods of time: Un breve antecedent (A Brief Antecedent, 1936–1960), La edad de oro (The Golden Age, 1961–1975), and Estertor del pistolero (Gunslinger Rattle, 1976–2006). Within this last classification, Núñez Marqués includes all the sound Westerns filmed in Europe until 2006, most of them Spanish-Italian co-productions. Altogether, there are 688 feature films: 31 were shot between 1936 and 1960, 598 Westerns were made between 1961 and 1975, and 59 movies were made between 1976 and 2006.[8]

The precise figures are not important; what is meaningful is the volume. In about twenty-five years, 31 films were made; in thirty years, 59 movies; and in fourteen years, 598! Indeed, the European Westerns filmed in the 1960s and the first half of the 1970s have their own prominence within the general history of Westerns and cinema.

In the beginning, the Spanish landscapes chosen for the Spaghetti Westerns were in Madrid or near Madrid. Art director Benjamín Fernández declared: "[Madrid's surroundings] . . . es el sitio donde más películas se han rodado en España" ([Madrid's surroundings] . . . are the places where more movies were filmed in Spain).[9] Already in the 1950s, *The Sheriff of Fractured Jaw* (1958) by Raoul Walsh was shot in Colmenar Viejo, and many more Westerns were filmed there, such as *Villa Rides* (1968) by Buzz Kulik, with Yul Brinner and Robert Mitchum. Madrid and its surroundings were converted into a big movie set where many Spaghetti Westerns (or "Gazpacho Westerns," if we accept Núñez Marqués's proposal) were filmed even before the Almería Westerns started to be shot.

In 1963, in Cerro de San Pedro around La Dehesa de Navalvillar, also in Colmenar Viejo (Madrid), a Western village, a fort, and a ranch were built by Augusto Lega and Félix Michelena, with the producer Emilio Lárraga representing the Cooperativa Cinematográfica Carthago.[10] Sergio Leone's *For a Few Dollars More* (1965) was mainly shot there, along with *Petroleum Girls* (1972), directed by Christian-Jaque, starring Claudia Cardinale and Brigitte Bardot.[11] In Hoyo de Manzanares (Madrid), another Western village was built. It was called "Golden City." Most of the film *A Fistful of Dollars* (1964) was filmed there. In fact, more than fifty Westerns were shot there.

In 1964, in Esplugues de Llobregat (Barcelona), another Western village was constructed: "Esplugas City." It was built by Estudios Cinematográficos Balcázar and served as the filming location for around fifty more Westerns.[12]

The first *poblados del oeste* (Western towns) built in Almería were in the Tabernas Desert: "Fraile" in 1965, "Juan García" in 1966, and "Tecisa" in 1966.[13]

Most of Sergio Leone's films, including *A Fistful of Dollars* (1964) and *For a Few Dollars More* (1965), were filmed in the surroundings of Madrid. *The Good, the Bad and the Ugly* (1966) was shot mostly in Almería's countryside.

But while Madrid was a big city with an airport and all types of facilities, "Almería at the beginning of the 1960s was one of the poorest provinces in Spain. It had the penultimate lowest per capita income of the country."[14] The province also had no airport and very few hotels. For Almería, the filmmaker's arrival meant almost a miracle. Enlightening and interesting in this regard is the documentary film *Spanish Western* (2014), shot by Alberto Esteban. Sean Connery declared his astonishment at the conditions Hollywood film stars had to endure: "The problem with Almería is that it has a problem of accessibility, and the accommodation is not as high-standards as other places in Spain, I have been."[15] They might have to spend twelve hours in a bus without air conditioning, driving on awful, small, and difficult roads from Madrid Airport to Almería, and, once there, the most luxurious place to stay was a three-star hotel where there were not rooms enough for all the crew.

The Spanish actor Álvaro de Luna remembers that time as a

wonderful chaos, as actors, technicians, and all types of film professionals were together there, a place that was for many of them "the end of the world," and, moreover, without understanding each other, as some spoke English, others French, others Italian, others Spanish.[16] It was like the Tower of Babel in the middle of the desert. It was frequent to encounter in the same scene two or three actors with different native languages. All said their lines in their own language, without really understanding what the others were saying, and then all of them were dubbed in the different countries where the films were released. But one way or another, they managed to make the movies.

In fact, these Spanish film professionals were very well prepared for their work, since, as the horse master Paco Anduras points out, when the Spaghetti Westerns were filmed in Spain, most Spanish movie professionals had already filmed many international co-productions, as they had already been trained by the Americans in the 1940s and 1950s. Anduras declared, "We were very lucky as we had the best masters of the cinematographic industry."[17]

The Spanish Madrilenian film director and script writer Joaquín Romero Marchent stands out with his Spaghetti Westerns *El Coyote* (1955), *La justicia del Coyote* (1955), *La venganza del Zorro* (1962), *Cabalgando hacia la muerte (El Zorro)* (1962), *Tres hombres buenos* (1963), *El sabor de la venganza* (1963), *Antes llega la muerte* (1964), *Aventuras del Oeste* (1964), *El aventurero de Gua-ynas* (1966), *La muerte cumple condena* (1966), *Fedra West* (1967), and *Condenados a vivir* (1972). Romero Marchent also directed some of the episodes of the Spanish TV series *Curro Jiménez* (1976–1978).

Another interesting Spanish film director who shot Spaghetti Westerns is Eugenio Martín Márquez, who filmed *El precio de un hombre* (*The Bounty Killer*, 1966); *El hombre de Río Malo* (1971) with James Mason, Lee van Cleef, and Gina Lollobrigida; and *El desafío de Pancho Villa* (1972) with Telly Savalas. He also co-directed *Réquiem para el gringo* (1968) with José Luis Merino.

"I have been killed more than 150 times in Spanish Westerns!" laughs the Spanish actor, Fernando Sancho. Álvaro de Luna, Fernando Rey, Paquita Rico, José Bódalo, Charo López, José Luis

López Vázquez, Mónica Rándal, Antonio Casas, Eduardo Fajardo, Marisa Paredes, Ricardo Palacios, and Emma Cohen are some of the Spanish actors who were present in those cowboy films that were co-produced and shot in Spain. We are only pointing out these few names among many other Spanish film directors, script writers, actors, and cinema professionals who did an excellent job filming totally or collaborating partially in most Spaghetti Westerns.

In Villa Santa Isabel, where *How I Won the War* (1967) was filmed with John Lennon playing a role, there is today a museum called Casa del Cine de Almería; it is in the town house where Lennon slept. There is also a Western film festival in Tabernas, the so-called Almería Western Film Festival (AWFF), where neo-Westerns are welcome every year and compete for the prizes in different categories: features, short films, etc. It usually takes place in the first fortnight every October.

And in Tabernas there are now three theme parks developed on the abandoned old Western villages, where nobody wanted to film anymore at the end of the twentieth century. They are Oasys Mini Hollywood, Fort Bravo, and Western Leone. They offer cowboy shows and a saloon with false film performances. They are places where one can spend the whole day living the experience of being in the Old West. As a mythic territory, almost legendary nowadays, Tabernas Desert in Almería is to European Westerns what Monument Valley in Arizona-Utah is to American Westerns.

The contribution that Spaniards made to the subgenre Spaghetti Western is such that they not only made many of them (with their land and their human resources, with their creativity and their work, as we have seen) but also gave the name to the subgenre, as "according to veteran Spaghetti Western actor Aldo Sambrell, the phrase 'Spaghetti Western' was coined by Spanish journalist Alfonso Sánchez."[18] In fact, the question of the name of the subgenre was in the air for a time, and it was also called "Paella Western."[19]

We see a common theme in all these proposals (Gazpacho Western, Chorizo Western, Paella Western, and Spaghetti Western): that, in any case, it was a Latin mixture, Italian and Spanish. Though being European, this modern Western was undoubtedly seen as mainly a creation of Southern European culture.

All these questions show how worthwhile it is to trace the Spanish and Latin elements in these international co-productions, shaping the character and form of these films. It is astonishing to see how all these circumstances have allowed the Hispanic and Spanish culture to be present not only in the roots of the "classical" American Western but also in the roots of the "modern" European Western.

It is surprising that despite such striking Hispanic-Spanish roots, both in the American Western and in the European Western, there are so few studies on this topic, for the reason that, if we are not aware of who we are and where we come from, we are destined to disappear, being swallowed by the prevailing trend.

## Paella and Spaghetti Western: Topics and Style

European movies are made with very little money. That becomes obvious when we watch them, and not only because of their aspect; it is also obvious that they are quickly made. Everybody involved in making those films had to do their work with little money, little time, and few resources.

We all know how important production is in films, and while American Westerns were generally filmed by the majors (Universal, MGM, Columbia, UA, etc.), the European Westerns were made by independent producers, mostly Spaniards or Italians, and most of them survived with difficulty within the film industry each time they made a film. Because of this reason we may state that European Westerns are playing in another league with regard to American Westerns, so they cannot be fairly compared if this question is not kept in mind.

As a consequence of this lack of resources, most of them are, in fact, not great films. They were not made to survive the passing of time; everybody knew that most of them were "flowers of a day." On the other hand, an average of 99.9 percent of *all* films disappear, and only 0.01 percent, at the most, survive as a masterpiece to be enjoyed by new generations.

It is true that many characters were stereotyped, and the plots were recurrent sometimes, but they kept the interest of the world fixed in the Far West, enjoying classic epic adventures and keeping an eye on the past, offering an alternative to the science fiction mainstream and the special effects cinema that has characterized the last decade's productions.

This continuity in the making of Westerns has had another consequence, as nowadays global generations, and, undoubtedly, the worldwide generations living during the second half of the twentieth century, have learned more of the history of the United States in the eighteenth and nineteenth centuries than of any other part in the planet.

Non-Americans know American nineteenth-century history better than their own country's history, in fact. Most Europeans, Japanese, Canadians, Australians, etc. know who the legendary Billy the Kid was, but few could mention any equivalent in their own country, and, for sure, in any culture there was a legendary bandit in those times. And all non-Americans know how people lived in the American Far West, but few know how people lived in the nineteenth century in their own country: the streets, the towns, the houses, the clothes, the names, the habits, the manners, the choices, the law, the families, etc.

These Spaghetti Westerns also have an outstanding quality: naturalism, which marks a difference from American Westerns. These Spaghetti Westerns are "dirty," full of "ugly" people with few resources, as it probably was in the original Far West, and quite different from the idealized image portrayed in classical Hollywood Westerns.

Some of these Westerns were soft, others brutal, but they all were made to be enjoyed, to entertain, and most of them achieved that, leaving a mark on popular culture. And contrary to what other genres dealt with, the main topic as a common factor that we can find in these films is the desire for justice, pointing out how the "bad guys" are always bullying the "good guys" and, in this sense, making an idealistic proposal for a better world.

To all the points already mentioned, we have to add that among these films some genuine jewels in the history of cinema appeared, for instance, Sergio Leone's films, which inspired Quentin Tarantino's Westerns and even his film *Kill Bill*, as he has declared, along with many other masters of cinematography.[20] These films represent the summit of Spaghetti Westerns. Considering all this, it is unbelievable that there are still people who disregard this subgenre.

The first Western filmed in Almería (in Tabernas and Cabo de Gata), before any *poblado* was built, is *The Savage Guns* (1961, known as *Tierra Brutal* in Spain). This film is credited as "the first Spaghetti Western," and it is defined as a "Eurowestern film."[21] It was a modest American—British—Spanish co-production. The film was directed by the British director Michael Carreras, who previously had worked for Hammer Studios. The plot sets the action in the Mexican state of Sonora, near Arizona Territory, in 1870. The Spanish actors Fernando Rey and Paquita Rico were among the protagonists. It was released in Spain in 1961, in the rest of Europe in 1962, and its American premiere was on October 1, 1962, with assistance from MGM.

This European movie already shows differences from the American ones. The main difference is not that the film is cheap, perhaps even cheaper than a B movie; the difference is that it is a philosophical Western, as we find that the protagonist, Steve Fallon (played by Richard Basehart), who is an outlaw who has killed people with his gun and is famous for being very quick with his revolver, does not want to fight. He just wants to be left on his own and not enter into quarrels, because he hates killing people. And the second protagonist, who is the owner of Ranch Buenavista, with views to the sea (supposedly the Pacific Ocean), Mike Summers (played by Don Taylor) is a former major in the Confederate Army, whose actions during the American Civil War have made him become a pacifist. Of course, it is quite unusual to find a Western where the two protagonists are reluctant to use guns and, moreover, discuss the question of whether it is forgivable or not to use a gun, even if you are attacked, considering the anguish that they feel when they kill someone. Of course, we have the wonderful *The Man Who Shot Liberty Valance* (1962) by John Ford, where James Stewart objects and denies firearms even for fighting the outrageous people who kill pitilessly, but this is quite an unusual American Western, and it was filmed a year later.

In *El vengador de California* (1963), also called *Il segno del Coyote* and in English *The Sign of The Coyote*, with a clear similarity to *The Sign of Zorro* (1958), we find an Italian-Spanish co-production filmed by the Italian director Mario Caiano, who specialized in Spaghetti Westerns, Peplums, and horror films. The author of the plot, the script, and the dialogue is the Spanish writer José Mallorquí, who is also the author of the novels and comics written in Spanish on El Coyote ("the prairie wolf") since 1943 with Editorial Molino. Mallorquí invented the fictional character that became famous, and later he wrote this cinematographic adaptation of his own writings. Coyote was an elegant California nobleman, charming and skeptic, but behind his facade he was a masked vigilante hero, a defender of the weak. He protected the original Hispanics and Native Americans from the Anglo-Americans, fighting for honesty, freedom, and justice. The protagonist is the Mexican actor Fernando Casanova, playing El Coyote/César de Echagüe, and the plot presents the conflicts in California in 1847 against the new US authorities (Governor Parker and Judge Clemens) and their unjust actions against the people, no matter if they were rich or poor Mexicans. Of course, El Coyote, like Zorro, will save them and their pride from the abuses perpetrated by "the Yankees." The novelty in this film as a Western is how explicitly the confrontation between Yankees and Mexicans in California is treated, dealing very carefully with their history, and mentioning Spanish and Mexican historical data with pride. For instance, they say, "Before British people arrived in America, Spanish had already founded universities," pointing out how the conquerors (the Yankees) were less refined and cultivated than the conquered (the Mexicans), and they show how the library of the former Mexican governor has books by Calderón or Lope de Vega, pointing out his good taste, though it is also stated that both governors, the Yankee and the Mexican, are corrupt men. Much real historical information is given in the film about the way the United States got California. Mexican landlords speak sadly and sourly of their land's fate: "Forty years ago this land was Spain, then it became Mexico, and now it is the USA," showing how lost they feel, without knowing who they really are and where their motherland is, their *patria*.

The Mexicans try to insult the Americans, calling them Yankees or gringos, and the Americans try to insult the Mexicans, calling them Californians or Mexicans. Racism is made obvious on many occasions along the film, a racism that is not against savage Indians, but against civilized former Mexicans. They declare clearly that they have been "invaded" (literally) by the Yankees, a conflict that is never related so explicitly in classic American Westerns. Again, the novelty of this Spaghetti Western is not how humble it is as a film production, but the approach it takes: how these American citizens are portrayed, what their concerns are, and what their "cultures" and conflicts are.[22]

The third example we are going to consider is *La cólera del viento* (*Revenge of Trinity*, 1970), a film directed by Mario Camus, a remarkable Spanish filmmaker who won the Golden Bear at the 33rd Berlin International Festival with *La colmena* (1982) and whose film *Los santos inocentes* (1984) won many other prizes and international and national recognitions, including the Best Actor Award at the 1984 Cannes Film Festival for its protagonists Francisco Rabal and Alfredo Landa. Since this film is directed by a Spaniard who is undoubtedly a skillful and recognized film creator, we ought to consider it even more than the others a Spanish Spaghetti Western. It is a Spanish-Italian co-production, and its main protagonist is Terence Hill (the Italian actor whose real name is Mario Girotti). What do we find here? The same scenario that we see in *The Savage Guns* and *El vengador de California*: a very cheap production with a different approach to the genre. In this case we find that this Western has a socially conscious approach. We find demonstrations of Mexicans at the door of the mayor's house asking for social justice (as in May 1968 in Paris), peasant protests, conspiracies, and secret political meetings to find a strategy to fight the villains. There is no sheriff; there is a mayor that keeps order with the help of the army, preserving US government interests. They literally speak of "explotados y explotadores" (exploited and exploiters), "libertad e igualdad" (liberty and equality), "hacer la revolución" (making the revolution), and "un nuevo orden social" (a new social order). The poor Mexicans (whose leader is the village teacher, who is killed by a paid assassin of the hypocritical landowner Don Pedro, played by Fernando Rey) also have class consciousness: they hate the rich ones who abuse them. Never in an American Western were these types of political questions raised.[23]

Finally, as another example of Spaghetti Westerns, we have *They Call Me Trinity* (1970), *Trinity Is Still My Name* (1971), and some other sequels. Both were directed by the Italian Enzo Barboni (who appears in credits under the pseudonym E. B. Clucher) and were filmed in Barcelona. In the same line, we find *Tedeum* (1972), which means "Of praise to God" and which was also released as *Sting of the West*, directed by Enzo G. Castellari. All of them are as cheap as all the other Spaghetti Westerns. They are Western-comedies, and they offer a parody. They show the decadence of the subgenre, and they have a certain resemblance (despite the obvious differences and degrees) to the American Western-comedy musical film *Paint Your Wagon* (1969, *La leyenda de la ciudad sin nombre* in Spain), directed by Joshua Logan. They are trivial and absurd, many times basic and crazy, but they were fun and provocative, good entertainment products, and very popular. *They Call Me Trinity* was the twenty-second most successful Italian film in 2004, one position below *The Good, The Bad and The Ugly*. And *Trinity Is Still My Name* was a huge financial success, becoming the top-grossing Italian film up until then, with 14,554,172 admissions in Italy.

Another novelty present in these films is how women, as a concept, are treated. For example, Mr. Summer, the wealthy landlord of *The Savage Guns*, played by the actor Don Taylor, is married to a Mexican woman, played by the Spanish actress Paquita Rico. The other Anglo-American character protagonist, Richard Basehart, falls in love with Juana, played by María Granada, who is Mrs. Summers's sister, and he decides to spend the rest of his life with her happily. It is not common to see this type of easy mixture in classical Westerns at the level of the protagonists of the story. If an Anglo-American Western landlord falls in love with a Mexican woman, many problems arise. An example is the wonderful film *Duel in the Sun* (nicknamed *Lust in the Dust*), directed in 1946 by King Vidor, where we find the terrible situation that the mestiza Pearl Chavez (played by Jennifer Jones) must face for the affair with Lewton "Lewt" McCanles (played by Gregory Peck). And, moreover, in *The Savage Guns*, Mrs. Summers, the Mexican lady, is a kind of Lady Macbeth, bullying her husband to fight and facing him sourly, quite an uncommon attitude compared with the quiet, supportive, and almost submissive married women who usually appear in American Westerns, especially if they are Mexicans.

In *El vengador de California*, the female protagonist of El Coyote is a "canonical" character, as Zorro's love interests usually are. But, again, as in the other film, there is an unusual female character: Lupita, a servant (played by Nadia Marlowa), who, as early as 1963, gets dressed in black as Coyote and with a horse saves him when he is in trouble. She is another quite unusual role, as she saves him despite being both a Mexican young woman and a servant, thus transgressing the double barriers of gender and social class.

In *La cólera del viento* (1970), the main female character is an attractive and beautiful businesswoman, Soledad (played by María Grazia Buccella). She runs her own *posada-taberna* (tavern-inn). Just considering the fact that she is a lone Mexican businesswoman at that time is quite an oddity. And she is a free, brave woman who faces the landlords, son and father, though she was abused by the father, Don Antonio (Fernando Rey), when she was a teenager. Mario Camus makes this character a symbol of how young, poor Mexican women are abused and how they survive. Even her name is a symbol: Soledad, "solitude." This character is another novelty who is quite unusual in the context of classical Westerns.

All these female characters offer another approach to the understanding of what a woman is, but, moreover, they specifically offer a new way of portraying Mexican women.

Another feature of these Spaghetti Westerns is the presence of sex in these films. There are more scenes with people having sex in beds, on tables, or wherever. We can see groups of villains treating women badly while abusing them, some of them being prostitutes, and some others ordinary Mexican wives or young women. We mostly see sexual violence against women and rapes. And the couples are not necessarily of the same race: we see Caucasians paired with Mexicans, Native Americans, etc. This is another Latin feature within the new Westerns, as sex is very important within

Latin culture (Italian–Spanish–Hispanic) in most of its expressions. In these European Westerns, for the good or for the bad, more sex is present.

Pointing out this mistreatment that women receive is another approximation to reality, as we can imagine how women were not safe surrounded by evil, stupid beings, closer to animals than to men, in the Wild West. These abusive and brutal men are very well portrayed by Sergio Leone in his Dollars Trilogy.

As we have seen with these examples, the significant difference between the American Western and the European Western is the approach. The difference is not only a formal question, as being dirty, ugly, and poor, or another way of filming with a new audiovisual language. It is also dealing with other topics, such as politics, history, morals, racism, and gender, showing how the Western genre was reinvented in Europe and adding new perspectives and new questions to our general understanding.

### Sergio Leone and His Films in Spain

Sergio Leone's film career could be divided into "before Spain" and "after Spain," as he filmed *A Fistful of Dollars* (1964), *For a Few Dollars More* (1965), and *The Good, the Bad and the Ugly* (1966), which is to say the whole Dollars Trilogy (also known as The Man with No Name Trilogy), entirely in Spain. This question "before/after" becomes obvious if we consider that in the first of these movies, shot in 1964, he wrote on the film credits that the film was directed by Bob Robertson, a pseudonym he invented, following the previously mentioned method of changing real names into English ones. They thought that these English names would benefit the film among eventual distributors, exhibitors, and audiences. Only a year later, in 1965, he signed *For a Few Dollars More* with his real name, Sergio Leone, showing that in only a year, with only one film, his prestige had grown so much that all knew that signing his film with his real name would benefit the movie, as a sign of its quality. So, thanks to these films shot between Madrid and Almería, he became recognized as an author and as an international director, being born for the world and for eternity.

With *A Fistful of Dollars* (1964), he had a budget of $200,000–225,000; with *For a Few Dollars More* (1965), he disposed of $600,000; and for making *The Good, the Bad and the Ugly* (1966), he received $1.2 million. His rise in barely three years was spectacular.

But Leone was not the only one who was born cinematographically in Spain. Ennio Morricone was, too. In *A Fistful of Dollars*, he appears in the credits as Dan Savio, a pseudonym also. Like Leone he only signed his music with his real name in the second film of the trilogy. With the first film, they felt so weak that in film credits they changed all their names into English ones, obviously for marketing reasons, and only after becoming strong—after being born for the world—did they proudly sign with their own names in the second and the third movies.

The only one who kept his real name among the "big ones" was Clint Eastwood. Of course, as an American he could. Nevertheless, he, like the others, was also born cinematographically in Spain.[24] With a playful look at the camera, Eastwood declared in the documentary film *Hollywood rueda en España (1955–1980)* that "*A Fistful of Dollars* became so successful, that it catapulted me . . . it 'placed' me."[25] Journalist Cristopher Hicks describes this moment:

> "In 1964 Eastwood was just another TV cowboy—co-starring in 'Rawhide'—when Leone cast him as the Man with No Name in his low-budget ($225,000) Western 'Per un Pugno di Dollari,' known in America as 'A Fistful of Dollars. . . . He was offered only $15,000 for the role. Eastwood naturally asked his agent why he didn't negotiate for more money. 'He said, "You'd better take it. They have Rory Calhoun in the wings." Well, I'd never seen Europe, so I decided to do it.' The film was scheduled to shoot during the hiatus between seasons of 'Rawhide.'"[26]

According to Wikipedia, "Eastwood was not the first actor approached to play the main character. Originally, Sergio Leone intended Henry Fonda. However, the production company could not afford to employ a major Hollywood star. Next, Leone offered Charles Bronson the part. He declined too, arguing that the script was bad. Other actors who turned the role down were Henry Silva, Rory Calhoun, Tony Russel, Steve Reeves, Ty Hardin, and James Coburn. Leone then turned his attention to Richard Harrison."[27] After Harrison refused too, the producers presented him with a list of available, lesser-known American actors and asked Harrison for counsel. He suggested Eastwood, "only because he knew how to ride a horse."[28] As Eastwood said in *Hollywood rueda en España (1955–1980)*, "So, they chose me because I was the cheapest one!" with another funny, mischievous look at the camera.[29] "It was a very interesting period in my life," Clint Eastwood said. "I like very much the people in Spain, especially those in Almería and around Madrid. They were so interested in the film, though nobody knew me at that time."[30]

Money was a problem; in fact, people from Almería told Antonio Lobo and Alberto Llamas that Sergio Leone, at a certain point of the shooting of *A Fistful of Dollars*, did not have enough cash to pay their expenses, and people in Almería were reluctant to give them more food or anything, or even to let them go, because it seemed that these Italian filmmakers were not as rich as the Americans and that everything was going to collapse. In these unlucky circumstances, his personal chauffer, Diego Fernández, seeing he was in trouble, offered to go for free to Madrid for money, and the people accepted, as long as Leone and his team would not leave Almería until Fernández returned.[31]

*A Fistful of Dollars* (1964) became a great worldwide success. The film made Eastwood an international star, Leone and Morricone were recognized as geniuses, and the term "Spaghetti Western" became an acknowledged and common phrase, gaining prestige and recognition as an interesting subgenre. All of them— Leone, Morricone, Eastwood—started this first film of the trilogy in quite amusing conditions, and, in less than three years of filming in Spain with the Spanish people, they all became international and recognized film professionals, whose goals changed the guidelines of the history of Westerns up until then. They always mention their work in Spain with respect and fulfilment, almost with a certain melancholy, remembering all the people who received them with joy, and always recognizing the enthusiastic and unreserved Spanish contribution to the films.[32]

Sergio Leone's pseudonym, Bob Robertson, is a testimonial dedication to his father, the Italian film director Roberto Roberti. His English first name for the pseudonym was Bob, the English nickname of his father's first name, Roberto, and his English family name for the pseudonym was Robertson, which is to say, "son of Robert."

Leone knew the Spanish land very well, as he had already filmed *The Colossus of Rhodes* (1961) in Spain. He crossed Spain by car, north to south and east to west, finding the most suitable sets for what he had in mind. He spent twenty-five days traveling by car around Spain before shooting.[33]

José Salcedo, Spanish director first assistant, commented that they filmed twelve hours a day and that everybody was exhausted, wishing for the sunset to come so they could take a break.[34] Sergio Leone usually woke up very early; his saying was, that if the team woke up early, he had to do it too, and he never went to bed until everything was okay. Leone wanted everything to be perfect, personally handling even the smallest details. Eli Wallach, the New York actor who played "the ugly" (a Mexican) in *The Good, the Bad and the Ugly*, remembers: "Leone knew each shot he wanted, and how he wanted it. He was very nervous, always worrying for everything, moving the fingers of the hand."[35] This finger movement was so constant that the Spaniards started calling him by the nickname "El Castañuelas" (Castanets).[36] On Sundays, Wallach remembers, "There were always soccer games, Italians against Spaniards, it was fun!" After work, some actors usually wanted a drink with the crew, but Eastwood used to go run for an hour, keeping fit.[37] Sergio Leone did not speak English, Clint Eastwood did not speak Italian, and most of the Spaniards around them did not speak either English or Italian. We will never know, within what must have been linguistic chaos, whether the fact that the Man with No Name did not speak much was a deliberate decision or something necessary within the circumstances.

In Alberto Esteban's *Spanish Western*, members of the film crew state that the cigar in Eastwood's mouth was a way to help him not speak (paradoxically, Eastwood is a non-smoker in real life)[38] and also a way of facilitating the dubbing in Italian and Spanish, as he was the only one who spoke English, as all the other actors in *A Fistful of Dollars* were Italian, Spanish, German, Austrian, etc., though they all appear in credits with English pseudonyms.[39] Nevertheless, Clint Eastwood has declared that he suggested to Leone that his character ought to talk as little as possible, as he understood and felt him dramatically as a non-talkative man, and that he cut some of his dialogue in the original script.[40]

Eastwood said that "producers complained about [my] seeming inaction on the screen. 'They said, "He's not doing anything. He's just standing there with that cigar in his mouth." They didn't understand the symbolism. Italian producers were used to a lot more dialogue.'" Eastwood added: "[Leone] had an operatic feel . . . a big, grandiose style. He was very big with the countryside."[41] "These European Westerns had a surprising concept," Eastwood said, "different with regard to the American Westerns of that time. . . . It was a new approach, fresh and new."[42] And Leone himself explained: "The type of Western that I make is the Western seen by the eyes of a European . . . as a foreigner can discover a country."[43]

No matter who had the ideas and what the reasons were, the director was Leone, a passionate man with a concept in mind, and he, like most authors and geniuses, was able to follow the main line of a piece of work and, at the same time, improvise, leaving the work flowing masterfully in his hands. His efforts and his thorough care to achieve masterpieces, no matter if he had to sign them with a pseudonym or not, were obvious from the very beginning and in the results.

He shot two more Westerns, partially in Spain: *Once Upon a Time in the West* (1968), which in 2009 was selected for preservation in the United States Film Registry by the Library of Congress, and *Duck, You Sucker!* (1971). The first one was shot in Italy, the United States, and Spain, and the second one in Ireland, too. He had a much higher budget, and, though they were close in time, everything was different.

With *Once Upon a Time in the West*, he counted on a budget

of more than $5 million, and he shot some interiors in Rome, in Cinecittà studios, and some scenes, such as the lynching of Harmonica's brother, in the north of Monument Valley. But most of the film was shot in Spain. All the scenes happening at the fictitious Cattle Corner Station were filmed in Granada, near Guadix in La Calahorra, and he built Sweetwater Ranch in Tabernas Desert, Almería. Moreover, the scenes that happened in the middle of the railway were also shot near Guadix. He had to bring red sand from Monument Valley, and he preferred to bring the sand than to shoot there, knowing Spain so well and not speaking English. He felt much more comfortable shooting in Spain.

*Duck, You Sucker!* (1971), also known as *A Fistful of Dynamite* and *Once Upon a Time... the Revolution*, narrates the story of Juan Miranda, a brutal Mexican outlaw, during the Mexican Revolution in the 1910s. The film was also mostly shot in southern Spain, though some flashback scenes were filmed at Howth Castle, in Dublin (Ireland). Sergio Leone presented the engravings "The Disasters of War" by Francisco de Goya to Giuseppe Ruzzolini, the director of photography, in order to demonstrate the desired lighting and color effects for the firing squad sequence.

He felt at home in Spain, since Spain was his cinematographic home. And this is meaningful again in terms of identity, as his films have these Latin identifying roots; he was an Italian, and the films were shot in Spain. This is to say that his films are the result of a work made by both Latin cultures (Italian and Spanish) together with the American one.

## The Fusion Antihero: A Blond, Blue-Eyed Cowboy with a Poncho

The Man with No Name is a postmodern Western antihero who is the result of the fusion of Anglo-American and Hispanic cultures. It required a European to create him. His silhouette is very different from the one we were used to seeing as the iconic Western cowboy. The Man with No Name, a tall guy wearing the conventional cowboy hat and boots, also has hanging from his shoulders a big cloth, a blanket, that reminds us more of a Mexican than of Wyatt Earp,

Billy the Kid, John Wayne, Gary Cooper, or any other mythical figure that inhabits our collective unconscious about cowboys.

He represents a fusion because, though he is a tall and slender man, dark-blonde-haired and blue-eyed, who wears a traditional cowboy hat, gun, and boots, he does not wear a small, fine waistcoat or a wide duster as customary cowboys do. Instead, he puts on a Mexican poncho, mixing features of both Anglo-American and Hispanic cultures. Undoubtedly, the poncho is a Mexican product (as the sombrero is an iconic symbol of Mexican culture). But the poncho, being Mexican, and meaning a fusion with Mexican culture, is even "more," as ponchos are also used by people from the Andes, and even from Patagonia, so we may say that ponchos are not only Mexican but also Hispanic, being, as it is, a worldwide Hispanic garment.

And, moreover, Eastwood in the Dollars Trilogy does not only wear a poncho, he also wears a peculiar, rustic, sheep waistcoat, without buttons and badly tied, a portrayal that puts him far away from the one we are used to seeing in the classical Anglo-American cowboy image with a well-sewn and fitted waistcoat. This is, again, another feature to bring us closer to Mexican culture.

But these two "marks" (the poncho and the sheep waistcoat) have something more implicit; they are not only Mexican or Hispanic symbols, but they are also a symbol of the poor people, the ones who have very few pesos and are the weakest. It is an image of the poor Mexicans, who traditionally are poorly treated in other Westerns or directly used only as part of the landscape.

Rich or important Mexicans rarely wear ponchos. Neither Zorro, nor Cisco Kid, nor Coyote wear a Poncho. Neither Emiliano Zapata nor Pancho Villa wore a poncho; if we observe their photographs, we see two men wearing suit jackets and sombreros. This is meaningful, as it means a double fusion in a hero: the cultural one between Anglo-American and Hispanic people, and the social fusion among poor Caucasians and poor Mexicans.

The paradox is that this poor Caucasian, played by Eastwood, is stronger than anyone because of his wit and skillfulness with firearms, yet even being the strongest—as we all know because he is always the winner in all the duels and confrontations—he chooses to dress humbly, as poor Mexicans do. But he does not really dress as a Mexican, as he keeps the traditional Anglo-American cowboy hat, boots, and spurs on, offering a surprising look and becoming a representation of pure fusion and modernity.

Undoubtedly, this well-known image of Clint Eastwood dressed wearing his cowboy hat, and his poncho pulled up, rolled on his shoulders, and his half cigar between his lips, conquered us and is ingrained in our brains. It is an image that is as powerful as the one we have of John Wayne dressed in a cowboy outfit, or Zorro, all in black, masked on his horse.

And this poncho, when he pulls it up for a duel, pulling the poncho backward on his shoulders, reminds us of science fiction heroes' capes, an image similar to Superman, Batman, etc., and Zorro himself, with their capes falling behind their backs, completing their silhouette. In those important moments, when lives are at stake, the poncho becomes a hero cape symbol. This mythical poncho worn by the Man with No Name was also made in Spain.[44] This is the only point on which everybody agrees. The poncho was Spanish: made, designed, and sewn by Spanish people.

Paco Barrilado (whose film pseudonym was Frank Barry) said to Antonio Lobo and Alberto Llamas that, one day, Sergio Leone unexpectedly told him: "Bring some ponchos." He got two hundred ordinary ponchos that were made in Níjar, and Leone chose one. Leone then told him: "Put something white near the neck to enhance the face," and they sewed the ethnic white designs that appear on it.[45] Carlo Simi, costume designer, on the other hand, declared that he was the one who decided that the Man with No Name wore a poncho.[46] And Clint Eastwood declared to the Spanish film magazine *Fotogramas* (January 19, 1979) that he had bought the poncho personally in Spain.[47]

Eastwood said that he had contributed to the construction of the character, making him less talkative than he initially was, as we have mentioned before, and that he had also bought his clothes: the hat in Santa Mónica at an ordinary store, the black Levi's on Hollywood Boulevard, and the cigars from a Beverly Hills store.[48] Then he brought to Spain the boots, the gun-belt, the cobra-handled Colt, and the spurs he wore in *Rawhide* (1959–1965).[49]

Whoever was the one who got it, the idea of a Western Caucasian hero wearing a Hispanic poncho was inspiring, showing how they were all a group of filmmakers in a state of grace, with a master ahead and a great actor facing the camera. And, in any case, all agree that the poncho was Spanish made and represented Hispanic culture.

The poncho is also meaningful structurally, as the trilogy starts, at the beginning of A Fistful of Dollars, with the first scene presenting the Man with No Name entering the camera frame in a village, riding a horse with his Hispanic poncho and his cowboy hat on. And in the last scene of the third film, *The Good, the Bad and the Ugly*, we see him disappearing into the horizon riding a horse and wearing the same Hispanic poncho and his cowboy hat.

Though the films were not thought of as a trilogy, the fact that the trilogy both starts and ends with Eastwood wearing his poncho and his cowboy hat, riding a horse, clearly is not a coincidence, if we are aware of Leone's meticulousness. It is a rondo, a circular structure, closing the circle of the movie adventures of the Man with No Name, whose character and identity are clearly defined by the fusion that his clothes express with this image.

And he, we, Leone, everybody, we all know that this outfit, this Hispanic poncho on this Caucasian cowboy, is a provocation to convention and to the classical concept of Western hero. This is why in the very first scene of A Fistful of Dollars, four cowboys laugh at him as he enters the town, because of his clothes, and they insult him and call him "scarecrow."[50]

We should note who else is wearing a poncho apart from him in this scene: the dead Mexican that has been killed and tied to the saddle of a horse and leaves the village with a paper on his back that says "Adiós amigo" in Spanish; the old Mexican, owner of the tavern, Silvanito; and the poor, cowardly husband of Marisol, Julio, who is pitilessly beaten. So, we have our hero, and then poor, or old, or dead Mexicans, all of them weak Mexicans, living in that wild society.

Eastwood's character dressing in such a way shows how brave and independent he is, mixing both cultures in his image. He offers a new image, breaking the tradition and mixing contraries. This is why he is provoking the four Caucasian cowboys that are on the porch at the beginning of the film. They see that he is different, and because of the poncho, they perceive him as weaker and laughable, and they insult him. This is why he has to face them, and not allow them to insult him, marking a limit, showing them who he is, no matter how he dresses, and finally he has to kill them. Thus, wearing a poncho can be a question of life or death. And all this is implicit in choosing all the narrative elements of this scene.

But the Man of No Name cannot be a hero because he has no principles. He is unpredictable: he may help you or he may kill you, and we never know what he is thinking and what he is going to do, whether he is going to save you or abandon you. For example, in *The Good, the Bad and the Ugly*, Tuco is always trying to guess whether they are partners, friends, or nothing, and every time he thinks that everything is okay and that he can trust Blondie (as Tuco calls the Man with No Name), the latter always abandons him (for instance, when he leaves him alone in the desert or after the duel when he disappears on his horse, leaving Tuco alone in the cemetery).

And he is a killer. He may kill four men in less than ten seconds because they called him "scarecrow" and they did not apologize. However, we also know that he may risk his life if someone moves him, usually the weakest ones, victims of injustices. And he also has a personal code of honor. He is not cruel; he is not brutal or a sadist, as many of his mates are. Neither a drunk, nor a dirty man, nor an offensive man. He is neither a liar nor a deceiver.

He sometimes acts nobly; for instance, when he helps Marisol, her son, and her husband to run away and, moreover, gives them money, in *A Fistful of Dollars*, or when he decides to destroy the strategic bridge, following the Union commander's wish, in *The Good, the Bad and the Ugly*. This is to disperse the Union and the Confederate soldiers, theoretically for having access to the cemetery, but really to avoid so many deaths, twice every day, when soldiers fight on the bridge. Leone portrays a pointless confrontation, making this scene a funny plea for peace. And the Man with No Name completes his good actions by comforting a young moribund soldier with his coat and his cigar. And, of course, the fact that he is, despite everything, "good" is explicitly stated in *The Good, the Bad and the Ugly*, as he is presented as "the good." He appears, for instance, playing sweetly with a baby cat, between death and prosecutions in the middle of a Civil War battle, in *The Good, the Bad and the Ugly*.

But, at the same time, he may abandon his mate in the desert, risking Tuco's life, after a little confrontation with him. And he kills men when he thinks he has to do it, without sheriffs' or judges' permission; he is an outsider of the system, taking the law into his own hands. All these contradictions lead us to realize that he is not a hero, but he is not a villain. He is an antihero, a modern antihero who represents a new understanding of our roots, mixed roots, as the Far West happened to be: a land of inevitable mixture. This unexpected cowboy, Eastwood with poncho, is a winner who always gets what he wants, and with his image and lack of prejudices, he speaks for two cultures that are many times antagonistic but in him reunited.

## The Spaghetti Western as a Postmodern Western: The Latin Western

The Man with No Name is a postmodern antihero for many reasons, not only because of his behavioral contradictions; the fact that he has no name is evidence of it. This anonymity is postmodern; it is ambiguous. He could be whomever, or perhaps all of us. And he is mysterious; we do not know anything about him. Who are his parents? English? German? Indigenous? A Mexican mother, perhaps? Spaniards? Anything may be possible. We feel close to him, but we do not know anything about him. We are ignorant even of his name. He may be known by nicknames that people around him give him, such as "Blondie" in *The Good, the Bad and the Ugly*, or "Joe" or "Manco" in the other two films of the trilogy, but nobody knows who he is, where he comes from, or where he goes.

This depicted ambiguity, added to the mixed clothes he wears, allows everybody to identify with him: Anglo-Americans, Mexicans, etc. And, precisely because of this ambiguity, he does not belong to any group, and none of them can say "he is one of us." Sergio Leone built this character with a scalpel, as a sculptor taking away everything that was not essential. The Man with No Name is minimalist; he has nothing, not even a name.

Leone's vision of the Wild West, together with the renovated visions we pointed out that are characteristic of the European Westerns, is a postmodern expression that in its beginning was disregarded and misunderstood. It is very sad that Leone died so young and had not seen the contemporary attitudes toward Spaghetti Westerns and, especially, toward his films. Currently, we perceive the obvious: that he, having deeply watched and studied American Westerns and passionately knowing everything about the classics, then turned the screw and went a step forward in creating new Westerns.

He made the *Plus Ultra* possible for Westerns, refuting those in the 1960s who thought that there was only a *Non Plus Ultra* for the Western genre, as though it was an old and exhausted genre, only suitable for old people or kids, and that everything was already said, done, and shown. He showed that with few resources you can make a work of art, showing how he could be classical and profoundly modern at the same time: something that is another postmodern characteristic.

Sergio Leone could see an old and abandoned *era de segar trigo* ("the mowing era," i.e., where the harvests are threshed) in the middle of nowhere and convert it into a mythical territory, as he did, for example, with the old abandoned "era" of Los Albaricoques (Níjar) in Almería, chosen by him to be the location where the legendary final duel among the three protagonists of *The Good, the Bad and the Ugly* was filmed.[51] Converting "trash" into "art" is another postmodern feature.

The films of the Dollars Trilogy are also well-known with their Italian and Spanish titles: *Por un puñado de dólares* (1964), *La muerte tenía un precio* (1965), *El bueno, el feo y el malo* (1966), and *Hasta que llegó su hora* (1968); and *Per Un Pugno Di Dollari* (1964), *Per Qualche Dollaro In Piu* (1965), *Il Buono, Il Brutto, Il Cattivo* (1966), and *Cera Una Volta Il West* (1968). This multilingualism is another sign of postmodernity.

Nowadays, we can say that all this fusion he revealed through thousands of details in his narratives, all these Hispanic symbols mixed with the Anglo-American ones that are present in his Westerns, are an expression of his vision of the stories that he imagined happened in the Far West. And, beyond that, they are an expression of the vision he had of the history of the United States.

With this vision and the way that he filmed, Leone proves to be not only a master of cinematography but also an avant-garde storyteller, a man of his time: a postmodernist. Richard Schickel writes on this topic: "In his introductory essay, Frayling firmly places Leone among the postmodernists, which is all right with me, since his films stress major post-modernist themes: They are self-conscious and knowing comments on the past; they are ironic in tone; and most important, they always emphasize style over substance."[52] We add that he portrayed fusion, ambiguity, contradictions, and mixture, as very few are able to do. He abandons the cannon and reinvents it, both formally and conceptually.

Quentin Tarantino has always acknowledged that Sergio Leone has been a profound influence for him, and in the 2012 *Sight and Sound* Directors' Poll, Tarantino included *The Good, the Bad and the Ugly* among his twelve favorite films. In fact, his films *Django Unchained* (2012) and *The Hateful Eight* (2015) are also postmodern Westerns. Tarantino declared that with *Django Unchained* he wanted "to do movies that deal with America's horrible past with slavery and stuff but do them like spaghetti westerns, not like big issue movies."[53] Obviously, Quentin Tarantino's title *Once Upon a Time in Hollywood* (2019) is also a clear homage to Sergio Leone's Western *Once Upon a Time in the West* (1968).

Clint Eastwood also professed his admiration for Sergio Leone and for his way of filming. He declared, "I'm sure he [Sergio Leone] influenced me a lot. His boldness, subject wise, and visually he was terrific. I admired his visual eye."[54] Eastwood dedicated his masterful film *Unforgiven* (1992) to Sergio Leone and Don Siegel.[55]

The Coen Brothers have also shot a Western, *True Grit* (2010), declaring that their favorite Western, among all of them, was *Once Upon a Time in the West*.[56] They say that "es el mejor Western de la historia" (it is the best Western in the history of Westerns).[57]

The Spanish filmmaker Pedro Almodóvar is another postmodern creator who asserts Leone's mastery. Almodóvar likes Spaghetti Westerns so much that he announced in 2020 that he wanted to film one: "Tengo un guion que es un western, está escrito y quiero hacerlo en Almería, en el mismo lugar donde rodó Leone . . . consistirá en un 'spaghetti western' donde la mayor parte visual y geográfica tendrá lugar en el Desierto de Tabernas. El título será 'Extraña forma de vida' y durará sobre 45 minutos." (I have written a script that is a Western, and I want to film it in Almería, in the same place where Leone shot. . . . It will be a "spaghetti western," where the most visual and geographic part will take place in Tabernas Desert. The title is "A Strange Way of Living" and it will last around forty-five minutes.)[58] Martin Scorsese also announced in 2020 that his next film would be a Western, whose title would be *Killers of the Flower Moon*.[59]

Sergio Leone, Quentin Tarantino, Clint Eastwood, the Coen Brothers, Pedro Almodóvar, and Martin Scorsese are the new Western makers who, after John Ford, Howard Hawks, Fritz Lang, Stanley Donen, King Vidor, Anthony Mann, Nicholas Ray, etc., have focused on new themes, plots, and ways of narrating that help us to understand and enjoy who we are.

In *Once Upon a Time in the West*, Sergio Leone is even more explicit with the postmodern fusion theme between Anglo-American and Hispanic cultures. It happens that, as in the Dollars Trilogy, we do not know anything about Harmonica (played by Charles Bronson), one of the main protagonists, except for his appearance and the final scene where we see him as a kid holding his brother before the brother was hanged. Though he does not wear a poncho, he is like the Man with No Name, as he wears strange clothes. They are almost-white clothes, a kind of "dirty white" color (most humble Mexicans used to dress in white at that time), and when he is introduced in the film, he does not wear a gun belt. And, when he plays the harmonica in the tavern-inn, he sits crossing his legs as many times Mexicans do when they sit on the floor. He looks and behaves more like a Mexican than like an Anglo-American, except that he is so tall and so self-confident and has blue eyes.

On the other hand, having blue eyes does not mean, of course, that you are not Mexican. Many Mexicans in Leone's films have blue eyes, such as Maria in *The Good, the Bad and the Ugly* and Marisol in *A Fistful of Dollars*. Significant pictorial representations we have of La Malinche show her carrying a blue-eyed baby, and she is sometimes identified as the first Mexican.

So, according to his appearance and manners, Harmonica could be Mexican or half-Mexican, and this is the big novelty: that this Western hero, Harmonica, is openly, because of all these features, Mexican or half-Mexican, and he is the equivalent to the cowboy played by John Wayne, Gary Cooper, Glenn Ford, Henry Fonda, Paul Newman, Steve McQueen, etc., all of them obviously Anglo-American Western heroes. The fact that Harmonica is played by an actor of Lithuanian descent, Charles Bronson (born Charles Dennis Buchinsky in Pennsylvania), does not diminish the Mexican or mestizo origin of his character, as Leone many times chose non-Mexicans to play Mexican roles. For example, "the ugly" in *The Good, the Bad and the Ugly*, whose character's name was Tuco Benedicto Pacífico Juan María Ramírez was played by the Jewish New Yorker Eli Wallach. Moreover, if someone were not aware of Harmonica's hybrid character, the final scene makes it clear, as the kid chosen to play Harmonica when he was a teenager is a boy who clearly looks Mexican, as his elder brother does.

And Harmonica is not the only one who is Mexican or mestizo, as Cheyenne is also supposed to be a Mexican, as his character's name indicates: Manuel "Cheyenne" Gutiérrez. He was played by the German-, English-, Welsh-, Irish-, and Swedish-descent actor Jason Robards, born in Chicago.

Harmonica, being mestizo or pure Mexican, is as Clint Eastwood's character was in the Dollars Trilogy: the postmodern cowboy antihero wearing a poncho. Harmonica is another Man with No Name. In fact, the role was first offered to Eastwood, but he had to decline because he had other professional commitments.

So, in this great movie we have two heroes/antiheroes who are either Mexicans or half Mexicans, and two Anglo-Saxon antagonists: Baron Morton (Gabriele Ferzetti) and Frank (Henry Fonda), who are the villains.

Sergio Leone's goals are many, more than we can give our attention to on this occasion, but, in his signs of identity, we cannot disregard the fact that he is Italian, which is to say, Latin. We all know that the Latin European countries are those whose languages derive from the Latin language, which happens to include the Spanish and Italian ones. Once more, we face the fact that the Latin trace in Westerns is much bigger than most people realize, as we are seeing how this subgenre, Spaghetti Western—filmed by thousands of Spaniards and Italians, and whose maximus exponent is Sergio Leone, an Italian—is, obviously, to a large degree, a Latin cultural expression.

### The Law of the Smartest: The Man with No Name as Lazarillo De Tormes

We have many times been told that the law of the jungle is the law of the strongest, and we may infer that, being that the Wild West was a kind of a jungle of wild outlaws and greedy people, this had to be the prevailing law. In fact, in most classical Westerns this is the rule, though what many times happens is that the hero, who looks weak, in truth is strong, as he is the quickest with the revolver. He then survives by destroying the bad guys and saving the vulnerable.

Well, one of the novelties that appears in Sergio Leone's narrative is that in his Western universe, the law of the strongest does not rule, but the law of the smartest. The Man with No Name is not only quick with his gun, he is also smart, very smart. He is surrounded by brutal men, "the bad," and by greedy egotistical liars, "the ugly," in *The Good, the Bad and the Ugly*. Or he is basically alone, as in *A Fistful of Dollars* (though not in *For a Few Dollars More*). And he survives, in all cases, because he does not believe anything he is told, and he never reveals his cards. He speaks the least and never says what he is going to do. We clearly see this strategy in the final duel of the third film of the trilogy if we consider the game of lies that the three duelists play as they try to discover what each other knows about where the money is. And we see how the Man with No Name creates traps to win the game.

He appears like a kind of gentleman among the ruffians that

surround him, one who has honor and does not betray, but then, unexpectedly, he subtly breaks the rules of the game whenever it is convenient for him. He wins not only because he may be the strongest or the quickest with his gun, but also because he has gone a step beyond his competitors, and he has created small traps to win—that is to say in the Far West, to survive.

We may say that our antihero, the Man with No Name, is a rascal, un *pícaro*, like the Spanish Literature Golden Age antihero Lazarillo de Tormes. The book, *La vida de Lazarillo de Tormes* (1554), tells the story of Lazarillo and is an icon within classic Spanish literature. Its genre, the picaresque satirical novel, is one of the strongest contributions made by Spanish culture to universal literature. And this character, and the book that narrates his story, is one of its summits.

Lazarillo is this type of antihero: a rascal that needs to deceive to survive, a person who has no rules, only his own rules, and who seems a nice person but can be very cold and cruel, too. He is a lonely wolf that is difficult to catch, who does not like to be violent or to harm people, but if he has to do it, he does it calmly and efficiently.

Everything that we have said of Lazarillo can be said of Eastwood's character. Sergio Leone Westerns are also satirical and masterful samples of picaresque.

But the Man with No Name has a peculiarity: unbelievably, he does not lie. He is so sharp that he lies without lying! How? Well, he wittily omits information, but he does not lie. For instance, when he is asked about the name of the tomb that the dying soldier confessed, he says "Arch Stanton," and it is false, but it is also true, as the dying soldier said, "The unknown tomb next to Arch Stanton's tomb." In fact, "Arch Stanton" was the only name given. The same thing happens with the stone, where he ought to have written the name of the tomb where the money is before the duel. As, being the tomb of an "unknown person," he could not write any name![60]

He, undoubtedly, is smart. And despite his methods, he is quite fair. He may not be the strongest, and perhaps he is not the quickest, but certainly he is the smartest rascal. And he is brave.

We have another good example of this at the end of *A Fistful of*

*Dollars*, when he saves his life in the final duel because he is wearing a steel chest-plate under his poncho that does not allow the rifle bullets to pass through! This is another trap. But, again, he makes a smart trap that is fair and understandable and that everybody applauds, as making this trap is the only way to survive in a duel with a revolver when the other duelist has a Winchester rifle. The Man with No Name hides a bulletproof vest as an answer to this injustice. It is the proper answer to survive a mean killer who uses a Winchester rifle without shame against a revolver in a duel.

The way Leone develops this idea is by following his many-times-used narrative resource: a rondo. He uses rondos with the structure of each film, with the whole trilogy, and with little themes, like in this case, where the steel plate that saves the Man with No Name's life reminds us of the old Spanish body armor that Ramón Rojo uses in his hacienda to practice shooting. Again, he closes a circle with this ironical paradox, as Ramón Rojo is killed by a man wearing a kind of an armor, as the one he uses in his hacienda with the purpose of training himself to kill people in duels with his Winchester.

So, making traps is another feature of this postmodern Western antihero, who wears clothes half-Mexican and half-Anglo-American and who, though a good person and a strong, skillful, and self-confident gunfighter, is a rascal, nevertheless: a "good" rascal. And this postmodern antihero loves money and spends his life looking for money. He does not want a family; he does not want love; he does not want a ranch or a house or a job; he only wants money and to be respected, and on his way in the search for money, if he can help someone, and if it is not too complicated, he will do it. And, as in the case of Lazarillo de Tormes, with the Man with No Name we all laugh and feel fulfilment following his unbelievable adventures.

## A New Audiovisual Language

Sergio Leone created, as the author he was, a new cinematographic style, almost a new language. It was more important *how* he was telling us than *what* he was telling us. The way he portrayed Spanish nature, finding beauty where others found trash, is so moving that it makes us rediscover already-seen places with new eyes. They do not only appear as beautiful landscapes, but they also become legendary. His wonderful shots led us to love what we thought we knew and did not really know until he showed it to us. Deserts, old houses, ugly ranches, abandoned villages, old carts and wagons, ragged clothes, filmed by him, these ordinary places and objects became mythical, mesmerizing us.

This fascination was deeply intensified by Ennio Morricone, his musical alter ego, his old schoolmate and comrade of adventures, as if they had been the Italian Huckleberry Finn and Tom Sawyer. His music completed Leone's work, and, like the songs of mermaids, it completed the enchantment.

Leone's ability to convert trash into art resembles Douglas Sirk's skills when dealing with melodramas, but in Leone's case, dealing with Westerns. Both genres, melodrama and Western, many times are disdained by prejudiced and pretentious critics and spectators. Both Sirk and Leone obliged these groups to rethink their standards, opinions, and judgments of what is good or bad in cinema history.

The position and angle of the camera, the chosen light, the way Leone managed the windows, doors, and even wholes to create his wonderful deep focus shots with black silhouettes, along with so many other cinematographic resources, were more than a language: they were and are a wizard's spell that he made with images, sound, and rhythm, the rhythm of each frame perfectly linked to the others, converting the dance of the photograms and scenes in a perfect operatic partiture.

His narrative was also made of silences. A film could start and play five or ten minutes before anyone said a word, yet popular audiences did not feel that they were watching a silent movie like the ones shot by Chaplin or Buster Keaton.

The heretical combinations he made, mixing extreme long shots with extreme close-up shots, and all types of pertinent forms, surprising us all the time with his unexpected but coherent camera movements, were also unique, the first of their kind. Later, they became canonical.

Christopher Frayling wrote in his book, *Sergio Leone: Something to Do with Death*, "Leone's images of showdowns and duels are still in the pantheon of visual clichés. Like Janet Leigh in the shower, Judy Garland on the Yellow Brick Road, Humphrey Bogart at the airport [in *Casablanca*] . . . they are instantly recognizable and can register in seconds. The French philosopher Jean Baudrilland called Sergio Leone 'the first post-modernist director'—the first to understand the hall of mirrors within the contemporary 'culture of quotations.' Thus, it is appropriate—necessary, even—that his work should have been since reflected by so many others."[61]

Leone sparked a whole revolution of the cinema language with his style, only comparable in intensity and effects to the one Orson Welles prompted with *Citizen Kane*. As the online commentator Korano remarked, "[Sergio Leone] is the man responsible for perfecting the Spaghetti style, and his contribution to the Spaghetti Western and Western in general is comparable to Orson Welles to film noir. A true *auteur* of film."[62]

We would need another book to deal with this question properly; here we only point out how meaningful this topic is. Unfortunately, Leone's edition of *Once Upon a Time in the West* was not respected by the industry, and shorter copies of the film with different lengths are shown nowadays in cinemas or on television, or offered on the internet. Sergio Leone's original version lasted 228 minutes. This original version was shown in Europe and was a box-office success, while the US-cut version was a financial failure. Sergio Leone was devastated by this manipulation of his work. "The strain of shooting the film in 1982–83 worsened an already serious heart condition, and the legal battle he endured with the studio in trying to preserve the film's 228-minute running time further eroded his health."[63]

Fortunately, *The Good, the Bad and the Ugly*, when it is shown as he edited it, is a precious treasure that allows us to thoroughly enjoy his style—perceiving his brilliant way of making Westerns—a style that has had an important influence in most later films shot by other great cineastes.

To conclude, we can consider, first, the masterpieces of the cinematographic art that have been pointed out all throughout this book, many of them being Westerns with powerful Hispanic heroes and antiheroes, as Cisco Kid and Zorro are, or hybrid Hispanic and Anglo-Saxon heroes, as the Man with No Name is. Second, we must also consider the uncountable recognitions made not only by the successive audiences to these feature films and TV series but also by international festivals and academies, including the Academy of Motion Picture Arts and Sciences (the Oscars). Third, we must consider the fact that Sergio Leone created a new cinematic language when shooting Westerns in Spain, together with mixed crews made up of Italians, Americans, and Spaniards. Fourth, thanks to this fusion of mixed heritages, both Hispanic and Anglo-Saxon, an unexpected and powerful, new, avant-garde, postmodernist Western narrative has emerged nowadays, with filmmakers like Quentin Tarantino, Clint Eastwood, Gore Verbinski, Pedro Almodóvar, Martin Scorsese, and the Coen Brothers, among others. Thus, we can state that the Hispanic roots of the Hollywood Western were and are meaningful and remarkable, and solid and fruitful, both in the beginning of Westerns as a film genre and all throughout the twentieth and twenty-first century, and both in Europe and in America.

# Notes

## Introduction

[1]William T. Pilkington and Don Graham, *Western Movies* (Albuquerque: University of New Mexico Press, 1979), 1.

[2]Charles Ramírez Berg, *Latino Images in Film: Stereotypes, Subversion, and Resistance* (Austin: University of Texas Press, 2002), 6.

[3]Francis M. Nevins, "An Aficionado's View: The Latino Dimension of the Hopalong Cassidy Films," *Bilingual Review/La Revista Bilingüe* 27, no. 2 (May–August 2003): 143.

[4]Quoted in Mary Lea Bandy and Kevin Stoehr, *Ride, Boldly Ride: The Evolution of the American Western* (Berkeley: University of California Press, 2012), 1.

[5]Ibid, 66.

[6]See George N. Fenin and William K. Everson, *The Western: From Silents to the Seventies* (New York: Grossman, 1973).

## Chapter 1

[1]Francis M. Nevins, "An Aficionado's View: The Latino Dimension of the Hopalong Cassidy Films," *Bilingual Review/La Revista Bilingüe* 27, no. 2 (May–August 2003): 143.

## Chapter 2

[1]We are well aware that the progenitors of the horse occupied this continent earlier in world history. However, the species unaccountably vanished centuries before the arrival of the Spaniards reintroduced it.

[2]In *The Broken Spears: The Aztec Account of the Conquest of Mexico*, the translation of one account of a battle tells of the death not only of the Spaniards but also of the "stags" that carried the "gods" on their shoulders. See Miguell Léon-Portilla, *The Broken Spears: The Aztec Account of the Conquest of Mexico* (Boston: Beacon Press, 1962).

[3]Frederic Remington, "Horses of the Plains," *The Century* 37, no. 3 (January 1889): 338, 343.

[4]Diana Serra Cary, *The Hollywood Posse: The Story of a Gallant Band of Horsemen Who Made Movie History* (Boston: Houghton Mifflin, 1975), 1.

[5]William T. Pilkington and Don Graham, *Western Movies* (Albuquerque: University of New Mexico Press, 1979), 2.

[6]Neil Campbell, *The Rhizomatic West: Representing the American West in a Transnational, Global, Media Age* (Lincoln: University of Nebraska Press, 2008), 3.

[7]Luis Reyes and Peter Rubie, *Hispanics in Hollywood: A Celebration of 100 Years in Film and Television* (Hollywood: Lone Eagle, 2000), 387.

## Chapter 3

[1]"Cisco Kid," Wikipedia: The Free Encyclopedia, Wikimedia Foundation, last edited April 22, 2024, https://en.wikipedia.org/wiki/The_Cisco_Kid.

[2]*Real Academia Española*, 23rd ed. (2014), s.v. "cisco," accessed June 24, 2024, https://dle.rae.es/cisco.

[3]José Manuel Rodríguez Humanes and Manuel Barrero, "Cisco Kid (1980, Vertice)"; Tebeosfera, 2008, accessed June 10, 2024, https://www.tebeosfera.com/colecciones/cisco_kid_1980_vertice.html.

[4]O. Henry, "The Caballero's Way," The Literature Network, Jalic Inc., http://www.online-literature.com/o_henry/1002/.

[5]Ibid.

[6]Ibid.

[7]Emilio García Riera, *México visto por el cine extranjero*, vol. 4, *1941–1969* (México, D.F.: Ediciones Era Universidad de Guadalajara, 1988), 32.

[8]"Cisco Kid," Wikipedia.

[9]Henry, "The Caballero's Way."

[10]Ibid.

[11]Raoul Walsh and Irvin Cummings, dirs., *In Old Arizona* (Los Angeles: Fox Film Corporation, 1928).

[12]Diego Cordoba, "A Western Masterpiece Is Back!," November 23, 2011, customer review of *The Cisco Kid*, Amazon, https://www.amazon.es/The-Cisco-Kid/dp/0912277009.

[13]Henry, "The Caballero's Way."

[14]John Dunning, *On the Air: The Encyclopedia of Old-Time Radio* (Oxford: Oxford University Press, 1998), 155–56.

[15]Edgar Morin, *El cine o el hombre imaginario* (Barcelona: Editorial Seix Barral, 2011).

[16]Terry Ramsaye and Ernest A. Rovelstad, eds., "The All-Time Best Sellers," in *The 1937–38 International Motion Picture Almanac* (New York: Quigley, 1938), 942, https://archive.org/details/international193738quig.

[17]Stephen King, *Everything's Eventual: 14 Dark Tales* (New York: Simon & Schuster, 2007), 26.

[18]Cortés, Carlos E., and Jane Sloan, eds. *Multicultural America*. Los Angeles: SAGE Publications, 2013.

[19]Lawrence Van Gelder, "At the Movies," *The New York Times*, August 17, 1990, accessed March 10, 2010, https://www.nytimes.com/1990/08/17/movies/at-the-movies.html?scp=83&sq=%22Twin+Peaks%22&st=nyt.

[20]Cortés and Sloan, *Multicultural America*, 506.

[21]Henry, "The Caballero's Way."

[22]Ibid.

[23]Walsh and Commings, *In Old Arizona*.

[24]Ibid.

[25]Henry, "The Caballero's Way."

[26]Walsh and Cummings, *In Old Arizona*, emphasis added.

[27]Henry, "The Caballero's Way."

[28]Bruce F. Kawin, ed., *To Have and Have Not* (Madison: The University of Wisconsin Press, 1980), 43.

[29]"Dogme 95," Wikipedia: The Free Encyclopedia, Wikimedia Foundation, last edited April 24, 2024, https://en.wikipedia.org/wiki/Dogme_95#Goals_and_rules.

[30]Deep Purple [musical group], "Hey Cisco," https://songmeanings.com/songs/view/3530822107858878944/.

[31]"Black Cisco Kid Jumpsuit with Red Shoulders," Elvis Presley in Concert, https://www.elvisconcerts.com/jumpsuits/1971-11.htm.

[32]War [musical group], "The Cisco Kid," https://genius.com/War-the-cisco-kid-lyrics.

[33]Don Williams, "Pancho," OldieLyrics, http://www.oldielyrics.com/lyrics/don_williams/pancho.html.

[34]Sublime [musical group], "Cisco Kid," https://www.musixmatch.com/lyrics/Sublime/Cisco-Kid.

[35]Malcolm D. Maclean, "O. Henry in Honduras," *American Literary Realism, 1870–1910* 1, no. 3 (1968): 39–46.

[36]"O. Henry," Wikipedia: La enciclopeida libre, Wikimedia Foundation, last edited April 24, 2024, https://es.wikipedia.org/wiki/O._Henry.

[37]Mark Memmot, "Obama Quotes O. Henry on 'Purely American' Nature of Thanksgiving," *The Two-Way*, NPR, November 23, 2011, retrieved September 26, 2013, http://www.npr.org/sections/thetwo-way/2011/11/23/142707934/obama-quotes-o-henry-on-purely-american-nature-of-thanksgiving.

[38]Francis M. Nevins, "An Aficionado's View: The Latino Dimension of the Hopalong Cassidy Films," *Bilingual Review/La Revista Bilingüe* 27, no. 2 (May–August 2003): 143.

## Chapter 4

[1]The irony of the fact that this most heroic of early Hollywood Hispanic movie heroes was created by Johnston McCulley, a New York writer, is not lost on us.

[2]Alfred Charles Richard Jr., *The Hispanic Image on the Silver Screen: An Interpretive Filmography from Silents into Sound, 1898–1935* (Westport, CT: Greenwood Press, 1992), 229.

[3]O. Henry, "The Caballero's Way," The Literature Network, Jalic Inc., http://www.online-literature.com/o_henry/1002/. There are any number of reprints of "The Caballero's Way."

[4]Francis M. Nevins and Gary D. Keller, *The Cisco Kid: American Hero, Hispanic Roots* (Tempe: Bilingual Press, 1998), 4.

[5]Fred Niblo, dir., *The Mark of Zorro* (Los Angeles: United Artists, 1920).

[6]Ibid.

[7]Donald Crisp, dir., *Don Q, Son of Zorro* (Los Angeles: United Artists,1925).

[8]William Witney and John English, dirs., *Zorro Rides Again* (Los Angeles: Republic Pictures, 1937).

[9]The DVD cover spells Yucatan this way.

[10]Witney and English, dirs., *Zorro Rides Again*.

[11]Ibid.

[12]Spencer Gordon Bennet and Wallace Grissell, dirs., *Zorro's Black Whip* (Los Angeles: Republic Pictures, 1944).

[13]Rouben Mamoulian, dir., *The Mark of Zorro* (Los Angeles: 20th Century Fox, 1940).

[14]Don McDougall, dir., *The Mark of Zorro* (Burbank, CA: American Broadcasting Corporation, 1974).

[15]Brian Garfield, *Western Films: A Complete Guide* (New York: Rawson Associates, 1982).

[16]Ibid, 382.

[17]Ibid.

[18]Ibid, 230.

[19]Martin Campbell, dir., *The Mask of Zorro* (Culver City, CA: Sony Pictures, 1998).

## Chapter 5

[1]Francisco Rodríguez Fernández, dir., *Hollywood rueda en España (1955–1980)* (Madrid: Sateco Documentalia, Radio Televisión Española, and TeleMadrid, 2017).

[2]Pablo León Aguinaga, *Sospechosos Habituales: El Cine Norteamericano, Estados Unidos y la España Franquista, 1939–1960* (Madrid: Consejo Superior de Investigaciones Científicas, 2010); Neal Moses Rosendorf, *Hollywood in Madrid: American Film Producers and the Franco Regime in the 1950s–1960s* (New York: Long Island University, 2017).

[3]Fernández, *Hollywood rueda en España, 1955–1980*.

[4]Fernández, *Hollywood rueda en España, 1955–1980*.

[5]Ibid.

[6]Ibid.

[7]Anselmo Núñez Marqués, *Western a la europea: Un plato que se sirve frío* (Madrid: Entrelíneas Editores, 2006).

[8]Ibid, 353–54.

[9]Fernández, *Hollywood rueda en España, 1955–1980*.

[10]"Decorados Dehesa de Navalvillar," Asociación Colmenar Viejo Tierra de Cine, accessed June 24, 2024, https://www.colmenarviejotierradecine.es/decorados-dehesa-de-navalvillar/.

[11]Ibid.

[12]Mari Carmen Gallego, "Esplugues recuerda sus años como plató de 'spaghetti western,'" *La Vanguardia*, January 20, 2014.

[13]Ibid.

[14]Alberto Esteban, dir., *Spanish Western* (Madrid: Albero Producciones and TVE, 2014).

[15]Ibid.

[16]Ibid.

[17]Ibid.

[18]C. Courtney Joyner, *The Westerners: Interviews with Actors, Directors, Writers and Producers* (Jefferson, NC: McFarland, 2009), 180.

[19]Christopher Frayling, *Spaghetti Westerns: Cowboys and Europeans from Karl May to Sergio Leone* (London: I. B. Tauris, 2006), xxi.

[20]Sergi Sánchez, "Kill Bill Vol. 2," *El Cultural*, July 22, 2004; Cristina Vega, "Kill Bill: Volumen 1: 13 curiosidades de la famosa película de Uma Thurman y Quentin Tarantino," *Sensacine*, July 4, 2017.

[21]Ernesto Garret Viñas, "El spaghetti western: La historia de un género cinematográfico que inspiraría a Stephen King para escribir su saga," *Revista de cine Mabuse*, March 2016.

[22]Mario Caiano, dir., *El vengador de California* (Madrid: Exclusivas Floralva Distribución, 1963).

[23]Mario Camus, dir., *La cólera del viento* (Rome: Interfilm, 1970).

[24]Joe Leydon, "Cover Story: Clint Eastwood's Unforgettable Stranger," *Cowboys & Indians*, August 14, 2017.

[25]Fernández, *Hollywood rueda en España, 1955–1980*.

[26]Christopher Hicks, "Eastwood Remembers 'Fistful of Dollars' Director," *Deseret News*, January 25, 1990.

[27]"A Fistful of Dollars," Wikipedia: The Free Encyclopedia, Wikimedia Foundation, last edited August 2, 2021, https://en.wikipedia.org/wiki/A_Fistful_of_Dollars.

[28]"Entretien avec Richard Harrison," Nanarland, September 18, 2012, accessed June 24, 2024, https://www.nanarland.com/interviews/entretiens/en/richard-harrison.html.

[29]Fernández, *Hollywood rueda en España, 1955–1980*.

[30]Esteban, *Spanish Western*.

[31]Antonio Lobo and Alberto Llamas, dirs., *Por un puñado de sueños* (Seville: Jaleo Films, Canal Sur Televisión, and Diputación de Almería, 2006).

[32]Fernández, *Hollywood rueda en España, 1955–1980*; Esteban, *Spanish Western*; Lobo and Llamas, *Por un puñado de sueños*.

[33]Lobo and Llamas, *Por un puñado de sueños*.

[34]Esteban, *Spanish Western*.

[35]Lobo and Llamas, *Por un puñado de sueños*.

[36]Ibid.

[37]Ibid.

[38]Ellie [pseud], "Cigar Smoking Icons: Clint Eastwood," *Havana House*, September 13, 2019, https://www.havanahouse.co.uk/cigar-smoking-icons-clint-eastwood.

[39]Esteban, *Spanish Western*.

[40]Fernández, *Hollywood rueda en España, 1955–1980*.

[41]Hicks, "Eastwood Remembers 'Fistful of Dollars' Director."

[42]Esteban, *Spanish Western*.

[43]Ibid.

[44]Michael Munn, *Clint Eastwood: Hollywood Loner* (London: Robson Books, 1992), 47.

[45]Lobo and Llamas, *Por un puñado de sueños*.

[46]Howard Hughes, *Aim for the Heart* (London: I. B. Tauris, 2009), 5.

[47]Paco López, "La historia del poncho de Clint Eastwood," *Anécdotas de Cine, Música y Arte*, July 4, 2020.

[48]Munn, *Clint Eastwood*, 46; López, "La historia del poncho de Clint Eastwood."

[49]Hughes, *Aim for the Heart*, 5.

[50]Sergio Leone, dir., *A Fistful of Dollars* (Madrid: Izaro Films, 1964).

[51]Fernández, *Hollywood rueda en España, 1955–1980*.

[52]Richard Schickel, "The Prince of Postmodern Darkness," *Los Angeles Times*, September 11, 2005.

[53]John Hiscock, "Quentin Tarantino: I'm Proud of My Flop," *The Daily Telegraph*, April 27, 2007.

[54]Hicks, "Eastwood Remembers 'Fistful of Dollars' Director."

[55]Leydon, "Cover Story: Clint Eastwood's Unforgettable Stranger."

[56]Matt Goldberg, "The Coen Brothers List Their 5 Favorite Westerns," *Collider*, January 7, 2001.

[57]D. Martínez, "50 Años del rodaje de 'Hasta que llegó su hora' en Almería," *Diario de Sevilla Cultura*, May 15, 2018.

[58]R. Pérez, "Pedro Almodóvar anuncia que quiere rodar un western en el Desierto de Tabernas," *ABC Andalucia*, September 4, 2020.

[59]Maria Aller, "La nueva película de Martin Scorsese será un Western," *Fotogramas*, February 19, 2020.

[60]Sergio Leone, dir. *The Good, the Bad, and the Ugly* (Los Angeles: United Artists, 1966).

[61]Frayling, quoted in Leydon, "Cover Story: Clint Eastwood's Unforgettable Stranger."

[62]Korano [pseud], "The Spaghetti Westerns of Sergio Leone," The Spaghetti Western Database, last edited January 9, 2011, https://www.spaghetti-western.net/index.php/The_Spaghetti_Westerns_of_Sergio_Leone.

[63]Dan Edwards, "Leone, Sergio," *Senses of Cinema* no. 22 (October 2002), https://www.sensesofcinema.com/2002/great-directors/leone/.

# Bibliography

Aller, Maria. "La nueva película de Martin Scorsese será un Western."
   *Fotogramas*, February 19, 2020. Año 73, n. 2116.

Aquila, Richard. "The Cisco Kid." In *Multicultural America*, edited by
   Carlos E. Cortés and Jane Sloan. Los Angeles: SAGE Publications, 2013.
   September, p. 106.

Asociación Colmenar Viejo Tierra de Cine. "Decorados Dehesa de Navalvillar."
   Colmenar Viejo, Tierra de Cine. Accessed June 24, 2024. https://www.colmenar-
   viejotierradecine.es/decorados-dehesa-de-navalvillar/.

Author interview with Paul Lazarus Jr. (former senior vice-president of
   Samuel Bronston Productions). Santa Barbara, CA, 1996.

Bandy, Mary Lea, and Kevin Stoehr. *Ride, Boldly Ride: The Evolution of the
   American Western*. Berkeley: University of California Press, 2012.

Barra, Allen. "Zorro." *American Heritage* 56, no. 6 (November/December 2005): 18.

Bennet, Spencer Gordon, and Wallace Grissell, dirs. *Zorro's Black Whip*.
   Los Angeles: Republic Pictures, 1944.

Berg, Charles Ramírez. *Latino Images in Film: Stereotypes, Subversion, a
   nd Resistance*. Austin: University of Texas Press, 2002.

"Borrador Previo para un Estudio Sobre Fines y Medios de la Propaganda
   de España en el Exterior." August 1960, p. 12. Archivo General de la Adminis-
   tración, Alcalá de Henares, Spain.

Browning, Mark. *Stephen King on the Big Screen*. Wilmington: Intellect Books, 2009.

Caiano, Mario, dir. *El vengador de California*. Madrid: Exclusivas Floralva
   Distribución, 1963.

Campbell, Martin, dir. *The Mask of Zorro*. Culver City, CA: Sony Pictures, 1998.

Campbell, Neil. *The Rhizomatic West: Representing the American West in a
   Transnational, Global, Media Age*. Lincoln: University of Nebraska Press, 2008.

Camus, Mario, dir. *La cólera del viento*. Rome: Interfilm, 1970.

Cary, Diana Serra. *The Hollywood Posse: The Story of a Gallant Band of
   Horsemen Who Made Movie History*. Boston: Houghton Mifflin, 1975.

"Cisco Kid." Wikipedia: The Free Encyclopedia. Wikimedia Foundation.
   Last edited April 22, 2024. https://en.wikipedia.org/wiki/The_Cisco_Kid.

Connor, Edward. "The Genealogy of Zorro: Deep Are the Reasons for the
   Perpetual Attraction of the Fop by Day & Robin Hood by Night." *Films in Review*
   8, no. 7 (August/September 1957): 330–33, 343.

Cordoba, Diego. "A Western Masterpiece Is Back!" November 23, 2011. Customer review of *The Cisco Kid*. Amazon. https://www.amazon.es/The-Cisco-Kid/dp/0912277009.

Cortés, Carlos E., and Jane Sloan, eds. *Multicultural America*. Los Angeles: SAGE Publications, 2013.

Crisp, Donald, dir. *Don Q, Son of Zorro*. Los Angeles: United Artists,1925.

Curtis, Sandra. *Zorro Unmasked: The Official History.* New York: Hyperion, 1998.

Cusic, Don. *Cowboys and the Wild West*. New York: Facts on File, 1994.

Deep Purple [musical group]. "Hey Cisco." https://songmeanings.com/songs/view/3530822107858878944/.

"Dogme 95." Wikipedia: The Free Encyclopedia. Wikimedia Foundation. Last edited April 24, 2024. https://en.wikipedia.org/wiki/Dogme_95#Goals_and_rules.

Dooley, Gerry. *The Zorro Television Companion*. Jefferson, NC: McFarland, 2005.

Dunnig, John. *On the Air: The Encyclopedia of Old-Time Radio*. Oxford: Oxford University Press, 1998.

Edwards, Dan. "Leone, Sergio." *Senses of Cinema* no. 22 (October 2002). https://www.sensesofcinema.com/2002/great-directors/leone/.

"Efforts of Motion Picture Export Association of America to Persuade Spanish Government to Liberalize Restrictions on United States Pictures." Box 2583 NND 95900, Record Group 59, US Department of State Central Files [RG 59], National Archives and Record Administration-Archives II, College Park, Maryland.

Ellie [pseud]. "Cigar Smoking Icons: Clint Eastwood." *Havana House*, September 13, 2019. https://www.havanahouse.co.uk/cigar-smoking-icons-clint-eastwood/.

"Black Cisco Kid Jumpsuit with Red Shoulders." Elvis Presley in Concert. https://www.elvisconcerts.com/jumpsuits/1971-11.htm.

Esteban, Alberto, dir. *Spanish Western*. Madrid: Albero Producciones and TVE, 2014.

Farinelli, Gian Luca, and Christopher Frayling. *La rivoluzione: Sergio Leone*. Bologna: Edizione Cineteca di Bologna, 2019.

Fenin, George N., and William K. Everson. *The Western: From Silents to the Seventies*. New York: Grossman, 1973.

Fernández, Francisco Rodríguez, dir. *Hollywood rueda en España (1955–1980)*. Madrid: Sateco Documentalia, Radio Televisión Española, and TeleMadrid, 2017.

Figueredo, D. H. *Revolvers and Pistolas, Vaqueros and Caballeros: Debunking the Old West*. Santa Barbara: Praeger, 2015.

"A Fistful of Dollars." Wikipedia: The Free Encyclopedia. Wikimedia Foundation. Last edited August 2, 2021. https://en.wikipedia.org/wiki/A_Fistful_of_Dollars.

"Francis (Given Name)." Wikipedia: The Free Encyclopedia. Wikimedia Foundation. Last edited April 30, 2024. https://en.wikipedia.org/wiki/Francis_(given_name).

Frayling, Christopher. *Spaghetti Westerns: Cowboys and Europeans from Karl May to Sergio Leone*. London: I. B. Tauris, 2006.

Gallego, Mari Carmen. "Esplugues recuerda sus años como plató de 'spaghetti western.'" *La Vanguardia*, January 20, 2014.

García Riera, Emilio. *México visto por el cine extranjero*. Vol. 4, *1941–1969*. México, D.F.: Ediciones Era Universidad de Guadalajara, 1988.

Garfield, Brian. *Western Films: A Complete Guide*. New York: Rawson Associates, 1982.

Goldberg, Matt. "The Coen Brothers List Their 5 Favorite Westerns." *Collider*, January 7, 2001.

Henry, O. "The Caballero's Way." The Literature Network. Jalic Inc. http://www.online-literature.com/o_henry/1002/.

———. *Puro Far West*. Translated by Javier Lucini. Sevilla: Mono Azul Editores, 2010.

Heston, Charlton. *In the Arena: An Autobiography*. New York: Berkeley, 1997.

Hicks, Christopher. "Eastwood Remembers 'Fistful of Dollars' Director." *Deseret News*, January 25, 1990.

Hiscock, John. "Quentin Tarantino: I'm Proud of My Flop." *The Daily Telegraph*, April 27, 2007.

Hoffman, Donald. "Whose Home on the Range?" *Melus* 22, no. 2 (Summer 1997): 45–59.

Hughes, Howard. *Aim for the Heart*. London: I. B. Tauris, 2009.

Joyner, C. Courtney. *The Westerners: Interviews with Actors, Directors, Writers and Producers*. Jefferson, NC: McFarland, 2009.

Kawin, Bruce F., ed. *To Have and Have Not*. Madison: The University of Wisconsin Press, 1980.

Kemp, Stuart. "Cannes: Quentin Tarantino to Host Screening of 'A Fistful of Dollars.'" *The Hollywood Reporter*, May 13, 2014.

King, Stephen. *Everything's Eventual: 14 Dark Tales*. New York: Simon & Schuster, 2007.

———. *Skeleton Crew*. Victoria: Penguin Books, 1986.

Korano [pseud]. "The Spaghetti Westerns of Sergio Leone." The Spaghetti Western Database. Last edited January 9, 2011. https://www.spaghetti-western.net/index.php/The_Spaghetti_Westerns_of_Sergio_Leone.

Lazarus, Paul, Jr. "The Madrid Movie Caper." *Focus* (University of California Santa Barbara) 16 (1995): 45–47.

Leen, Catherine. "The Caballero Revisited: Postmodernity in *The Cisco Kid*, *The Mask of Zorro*, and *Shrek II*." *Bilingual Review/La Revista Bilingüe* 28, no. 1 (January 2004–April 2007): 23–35.

León Aguinaga, Pablo. *Sospechosos Habituales: El Cine Norteamericano, Estados Unidos y la España Franquista, 1939–1960*. Madrid: Consejo Superior de Investigaciones Científicas, 2010.

Leone, Sergio, dir. *A Fistful of Dollars*. Madrid: Izaro Films, 1964.

———. *For a Few Dollars More*. Los Angeles: United Artists, 1965.

———. *The Good, the Bad, and the Ugly*. Los Angeles: United Artists, 1966.

Léon-Portilla, Miguell. *The Broken Spears: The Aztec Account of the Conquest of Mexico*. Boston: Beacon Press, 1962.

Leydon, Joe. "Cover Story: Clint Eastwood's Unforgettable Stranger." *Cowboys & Indians*, August 14, 2017.

Lobo, Antonio, and Alberto Llamas, dirs. *Por un puñado de sueños*. Seville: Jaleo Films, Canal SurTelevisión, and Diputación de Almería, 2006.

López, Paco. "La historia del poncho de Clint Eastwood." *Anécdotas de Cine, Música y Arte*, July 4, 2020.

Maclean, Malcolm D. "O. Henry in Honduras." *American Literary Realism, 1870–1910* 1, no. 3 (1968): 39–46.

Mamoulian, Rouben, dir. *The Mark of Zorro*. Los Angeles: 20th Century Fox, 1940.

Martínez, D. "50 Años del rodaje de 'Hasta que llegó su hora' en Almería." *Diario de Sevilla Cultura*, May 15, 2018.

McDougall, Don, dir. *The Mark of Zorro*. Burbank, CA: American Broadcasting Corporation, 1974.

Memmot, Mark. "Obama Quotes O. Henry on 'Purely American' Nature of Thanksgiving." *The Two-Way*, NPR, November 23, 2011. Retrieved September 26, 2013. http://www.npr.org/sections/thetwo-way/2011/11/23/142707934/obama-quotes-o-henry-on-purely-american-nature-of-thanksgiving.

"Michael Connelly." Wikipedia: The Free Encyclopedia. Wikimedia Foundation. Last edited May 7, 2024. https://en.wikipedia.org/wiki/Michael_Connelly.

Morin, Edgar. *El cine o el hombre imaginario*. Barcelona: Editorial Seix Barral, 2011.

Munn, Michael. *Clint Eastwood: Hollywood Loner*. London: Robson Books, 1992.

Murcia, Fran. "Escenarios de cine en Almería para adentrarse en una película." *Diario de Almería*. Grupo Joly. 2019. https://www.diariodealmeria.es/temas/localizaciones-cine-almeria-peliculas/index.php#Rincon-9.

Nanarland. "Entretien avec Richard Harrison." Nanarland, September 18, 2012. Accessed June 24, 2024. https://www.nanarland.com/interviews/entretiens/en/richard-harrison.html.

Núñez Marqués, Anselmo. *Western a la europea: Un plato que se sirve frío*. Madrid: Entrelíneas Editores, 2006.

Nevins, Francis M. "An Aficionado's View: The Latino Dimension of the Hopalong Cassidy Films." *Bilingual Review/La Revista Bilingüe* 27, no. 2 (May–August 2003): 143–58.

Nevins, Francis M., and Gary D. Keller. *The Cisco Kid: American Hero, Hispanic Roots*. Tempe: Bilingual Press, 1998.

Niblo, Fred, dir. *The Mark of Zorro*. Los Angeles: United Artists, 1920.

Noriega, Chon A. "The Western's 'Forgotten People.'" *Aztlán: A Journal of Chicano Studies* 34, no. 1 (Spring 2009): 1–9.

"O. Henry." Wikipedia: La enciclopeida libre. Wikimedia Foundation. Last edited April 24, 2024. https://es.wikipedia.org/wiki/O._Henry.

Pérez, R. "Pedro Almodóvar anuncia que quiere rodar un western en el Desierto de Tabernas." *ABC Andalucia*, September 4, 2020.

"Per un pugno di dollari – Box Office Data, DVD Sales, Movie News, Cast Information." *The Numbers*. Nash Information Services, LLC. Retrieved July 11, 2021. https://www.the-numbers.com/movie/Per-un-pugno-di-dollari#tab=summary.

Pilkington, William T., and Don Graham. *Western Movies*. Albuquerque: University of New Mexico Press, 1979.

Preston, Paul. *Franco: A Biography*. New York: HarperCollins, 1995.

———. *Juan Carlos: Steering Spain from Dictatorship to Democracy*. New York: Norton, 2004.

Ramsaye, Terry, and Ernest A. Rovelstad, eds. "The All-Time Best Sellers." In *The 1937–38 International Motion Picture Almanac*, vol. 1, 942. New York: Quigley, 1938. https://archive.org/details/international193738quig.

Remington, Frederic. "Horses of the Plains." *The Century* 37, no. 3 (January 1889): 332–43.

Reyes, Luis, and Peter Rubie. *Hispanics in Hollywood: A Celebration of 100 Years in Film and Television*. Hollywood: Lone Eagle, 2000.

Richard, Alfred Charles, Jr. *The Hispanic Image on the Silver Screen: An Interpretive Filmography from Silents into Sound, 1898–1935*. Westport, CT: Greenwood Press, 1992.

Rodríguez Humanes, José Manuel, and Manuel Barrero. "Cisco Kid (1980, Vertice)." *Tebeosfera*. 2008. Accessed June 10, 2024. https://www.tebeosfera.com/colecciones/cisco_kid_1980_vertice.html.

Rosendorf, Neal Moses. *Hollywood in Madrid: American Film Producers and the Franco Regime in the 1950s–1960s*. New York: Long Island University, 2017.

Sánchez, Sergi. "Kill Bill Vol. 2." *El Cultural*, July 22, 2004.

Schickel, Richard. "The Prince of Postmodern Darkness." *Los Angeles Times*, September 11, 2005. https://www.latimes.com/archives/la-xpm-2005-sep-11-bk-schickel11-story.html

Spring, Katherine. *Saying It with Songs: Popular Music and the Coming of Sound to Hollywood Cinema*. New York: Oxford University Press, 2013.

Studio 360. "Quentin Tarantino: Once upon a time... in cinema." *The World (PRX)*, February 6, 2020.

Sublime [musical group]. "Cisco Kid." https://www.musixmatch.com/lyrics/Sublime/Cisco-Kid.

"Testimony of Samuel Bronston." June 24, 1966, pp. 8–17, in *Bankruptcy of Samuel Bronston*, 64 B 464, US District Court, New York City. In author's collection (files originally stored in NARA facility, Lee's Summit, MO, but subsequently destroyed as per standard policy).

"Top Italian Film Grossers." *Variety*, October 11, 1967.

Van Gelder, Lawrence. "At the Movies." *The New York Times*, August 17, 1990. Retrieved March 10, 2010. https://www.nytimes.com/1990/08/17/movies/at-the-movies.html?scp=83&sq=%22Twin+Peaks%22&st=nyt.

Vega, Cristina. "Kill Bill: Volumen 1: 13 curiosidades de la famosa película de Uma Thurman y Quentin Tarantino." *Sensacine*, July 4, 2017.

Viñas, Ernesto Garret. "El spaghetti western: La historia de un género cinematográfico que inspiraría a Stephen King para escribir su saga." *Revista de cine Mabuse*, March 2016.

Walsh, Raoul, and Irvin Cummings, dirs. *In Old Arizona*. Los Angeles: Fox Film Corporation, 1928.

War [musical group] "The Cisco Kid." https://genius.com/War-the-cisco-kid-lyrics.

Williams, Don. "Pancho." OldieLyrics. http://www.oldielyrics.com/lyrics/don_williams/pancho.html.

Witney, William, and John English, dirs. *Zorro Rides Again*. Los Angeles: Republic Pictures, 1937.

Yoggy, Gary. *Riding the Video Range: The Rise and Fall of the Western on Television*. Jefferson, NC: McFarland, 2008.

# Index